Focus in High School Mathematics:
Fostering Reasoning and
Sense Making for All Students

Edited by

Marilyn E. Strutchens
Auburn University
Auburn, Alabama

Judith Reed Quander
University of Houston—Downtown
Houston, Texas

NATIONAL COUNCIL OF
TEACHERS OF MATHEMATICS

Copyright © 2011 by
The National Council of Teachers of Mathematics, Inc.
1906 Association Drive, Reston, VA 20191-1502
(703) 620-9840; (800) 235-7566; www.nctm.org
All rights reserved

Library of Congress Cataloging-in-Publication Data

Focus in high school mathematics. Fostering reasoning and sense making
for all students / edited by Marilyn E. Strutchens and Judith Reed
Quander.
    p. cm.
  ISBN 978-0-87353-680-6
  1. Mathematics—Study and teaching (Secondary)—United States. 2.
Curriculum planning—United States. I. Strutchens, Marilyn E., 1962–
II. Quander, Judith Reed. III. Title: Fostering reasoning and sense
making for all students.
  QA13.F633 2011
  510.071′2—dc22
                        2010050758

The National Council of Teachers of Mathematics is a public voice of mathematics
education, supporting teachers to ensure equitable mathematics learning of the
highest quality for all students through vision, leadership, professional development,
and research.

Printed in the United States of America

Contents

Preface

Focus in High School Mathematics: Reasoning and Sense Making (NCTM 2009) captures the direction for high school mathematics for students in the twenty-first century:

> Reasoning and sense making should occur in every mathematics classroom every day. In such an environment, teachers and students ask and answer such questions as "What's going on here?" and "Why do you think that?" Addressing reasoning and sense making does not need to be an extra burden for teachers struggling with students who are having a difficult time just learning the procedures. On the contrary, the structure that reasoning brings forms a vital support for understanding and continued learning. Currently, many students have difficulty because they find mathematics meaningless. . . .
> With purposeful attention and planning, teachers can hold all students in every high school mathematics classroom accountable for personally engaging in reasoning and sense making, and thus lead students to experience reasoning for themselves rather than merely observe it. (NCTM 2009, pp. 5–6)

This new publication urges a refocusing of the high school mathematics curriculum on reasoning and sense making, building on the guidelines for teaching and learning mathematics advocated by NCTM in *Principles and Standards for School Mathematics* (NCTM 2000). *Focus in High School Mathematics: Reasoning and Sense Making* makes the case that reasoning and sense making must reside at the core of all mathematics learning and instruction, at all grades. Moving forward from *Curriculum Focal Points for Prekindergarten through Grade 8 Mathematics* (NCTM 2006), *Focus in High School Mathematics: Reasoning and Sense Making* also addresses the need for the continuation of a coherent and well-articulated mathematics curriculum at the high school level.

The underlying principles of *Focus in High School Mathematics: Reasoning and Sense Making* are "reasoning habits" that should develop across the curriculum, along with "key elements" organized around five content strands. The book provides a group of examples that illustrate how these principles might play out in the classroom. Historically, NCTM has provided supplementary materials to accompany major publications that present official positions of the Council (e.g., Teaching with Curriculum Focal Points for *Curriculum Focal Points for Prekindergarten through Grade 8 Mathematics,* the Navigations Series for *Principles and Standards for School Mathematics*, the Addenda Series for *Curriculum and Evaluation Standards for School Mathematics* [NCTM 1989]). In keeping with this tradition, a series of supplementary books, Focus in High School Mathematics, offers additional guidance for ensuring that reasoning and sense making are part of the mathematics experiences of all high school students every day.

This series is intended for secondary mathematics teachers, curriculum specialists, mathematics supervisors, district administrators, and mathematics teacher educators. *Focus in High School Mathematics: Reasoning and Sense Making* underscores the critical role of the Process Standards outlined in *Principles and Standards* and provides a foundation for as achieving the principal goals for the mathematical experiences of all secondary school students. Each volume in the Focus in High School Mathematics series presents detailed examples of worthwhile mathematical tasks, along with follow-up discussion. The examples and discussions are intended to help classroom teachers understand what it means to promote sense making and to find ways to increase it in their classrooms. The material could also be used as classroom cases in professional development. In addition, supervisors, curriculum specialists, and administrators might use the examples and discussions to catalyze conversations about shifts in the high school mathematics curriculum to bring them into alignment with the goals of *Focus in High School Mathematics: Reasoning and Sense Making*.

Although the books in the series focus on a particular content strand or principle of school mathematics identified in *Principles and Standards*, they are not intended to outline a curriculum for a particular area or topic. In fact, many of the examples in the books point to potential connections across content areas and ideas.

General Introduction to the Focus in High School Mathematics Series

Focus in High School Mathematics: Reasoning and Sense Making addresses the need for reasoning to play a larger role in high school mathematics:

> A focus on reasoning and sense making, when developed in the context of strong content, will ensure that students can accurately carry out mathematical procedures, understand why those procedures work, and know how they might be used and their results interpreted. . . . Such a focus on reasoning and sense making will produce citizens who make informed and reasoned decisions, including quantitatively sophisticated choices about their personal finances, about which public policies deserve their support, and about which insurance or health plans to select. It will also produce workers who can satisfy the increased mathematical needs in professional areas ranging from health care to small business to digital technology. (NCTM 2009, p. 3)

Focus in High School Mathematics: Reasoning and Sense Making outlines how reasoning and sense making might play out in core topic areas of the high school curriculum: numbers and measurement, algebra, geometry, and statistics and probability. The topics and examples contained in this publication and the supporting volumes do not represent an exhaustive list of topics that should be covered in any particular course or curriculum. The examples are meant to illustrate reasoning habits that all students at a variety of grade levels should know by the time they complete high school. As such, they provide multiple entry points for the students and, where appropriate, emphasize connections between several areas of mathematics. The discussions point to key teaching strategies that foster the development of reasoning and sense making. The strategies should be viewed as general and not tied to the particular context or task.

Most teachers and teacher educators would probably nod in agreement that reasoning and sense making are important to consider in the mathematical experiences of their students. However, the purpose of *Focus in High School Mathematics: Reasoning and Sense Making* and the Focus in High School Mathematics series is to highlight these as major goals of the study of secondary mathematics. Although reasoning and sense making may have been a part of secondary mathematics teaching and learning in the past, they are certainly worthy of being discussed in greater depth, and becoming a primary focus of our secondary mathematics teaching, in classrooms today. Therefore, with this shift in emphasis, it is important for NCTM to provide thoughtful examples of worthwhile tasks that can be pursued at several levels.

The Role of Teaching

Often, high school mathematics teaching in the United States and Canada has been characterized by two main classroom activities: teachers share information, such as definitions of new terms and procedures for solving mathematics problems, and then students practice and perhaps discuss results of those procedures. Although these activities are important, such practices can lead to learning that is devoid of reasoning and sense making. By contrast, NCTM strongly supports a view of mathematics teaching and learning that focuses on reasoning, as described in *Mathematics Teaching Today* (NCTM 2007): "Teachers . . . must shift their perspectives about teaching from that of a process of delivering information to that of a process of facilitating students' sense making about mathematics" (p. 5).

A shift of perspective to one that views reasoning and sense making as primary goals for students' learning of mathematics will lead to a shift in choices made by the classroom teacher. For example, the teacher will choose tasks that allow students to see the need for sense making and give them opportunities to demonstrate their reasoning processes. Such tasks should also help students build on their informal knowledge of mathematics and see the logical connections with other areas of mathematics that they have learned. This shift may require changes in the structure of the classroom setting so that students are challenged and encouraged to explore mathematical situations both collaboratively and independently. Students should be expected to make conjectures and develop arguments to support them, connecting earlier knowledge with newly acquired knowledge.

As students are investigating and shaping ideas, they should have opportunities to interact directly and openly with one another and with the teacher. More details about the teacher's and students' roles in the classroom can be found in chapter 1, "Standards for Teaching and Learning," of *Mathematics Teaching Today* (NCTM 2007), which includes Standards describing characteristics of *worthwhile mathematical tasks* (Standard 3), components of a productive classroom *learning environment* (Standard 4), and suggestions for orchestrating mathematical *discourse* (Standard 5). The Focus in High School Mathematics series furnishes tasks, examples, and classroom vignettes that illustrate how a teacher might choose tasks and orchestrate classroom discourse to capitalize on student reasoning and promote sense making.

The Role of Technology

In all of the books in the series, technology is integrated into the examples in a strategic manner to enrich opportunities for students' reasoning and sense making. The power of recent technological tools (e.g., computer algebra systems, dynamic geometry software, and dynamic data representation tools) to enhance reasoning and sense making in mathematics is so great that omitting them from these volumes would be remiss.

Increasingly, technology is an integral part of society and the research conducted in most mathematics-related fields. The series supports the philosophy of *Focus in High School Mathematics: Reasoning and Sense Making* that "students can be challenged to take responsibility for deciding which tool might be useful in a given situation when they are allowed to choose from a menu of mathematical tools that includes technology. Students who have regular opportunities to discuss and reflect on how a technological tool is used effectively will be less apt to use technology as a crutch" (NCTM 2009, p. 14).

All the companion volumes in the Focus in High School Mathematics series offer examples that show students using technology to reduce computational overhead, while also illustrating the use of technology in experimenting with mathematical objects and modeling mathematical structures. However, NCTM has long recognized the special importance of technology in school mathematics, as expressed in the Technology Principle in *Principles and Standards*. Mathematics education of the highest quality must support students in using technology effectively and confidently. Accordingly, the series develops the topic of technology in a separate volume that highlights the power of technology to assist and advance students' efforts to reason about and make sense of mathematics in grades 9–12.

The Format of the Focus in High School Mathematics Series

Focus in High School Mathematics: Reasoning and Sense Making underscores the need to refocus the high school mathematics curriculum on reasoning and sense making. The companion books offer further insights into how these ways of thinking might develop in other major areas of content in high school mathematics:

- *Focus in High School Mathematics: Reasoning and Sense Making in Algebra*
- *Focus in High School Mathematics: Reasoning and Sense Making in Geometry*

- *Focus in High School Mathematics: Reasoning and Sense Making in Statistics and Probability*
- *Focus in High School Mathematics: Fostering Reasoning and Sense Making for All Students*

The strand on reasoning and sense making with numbers and measurement discussed in *Focus in High School Mathematics: Reasoning and Sense Making* receives primary attention in *Focus in High School Mathematics: Geometry,* but other books also address aspects of this strand.

Additional volumes in the Focus in High School Mathematics series develop ideas related to important principles of school mathematics identified in *Principles and Standards.* As noted above, a volume highlighting the use of technology to reason about and make sense of mathematics supports the Technology Principle.

However, no consideration of reasoning and sense making in high school mathematics can be complete without devoting attention to equal treatment of students, regardless of talent, background, and personal advantages or disadvantages of many sorts. All high school students must have a chance to reason about and make sense of mathematics in significant ways. Thus, the series includes a volume that highlights equitable opportunities for reasoning and sense making, lending support to the Equity Principle set forth in *Principles and Standards.*

Reasoning Habits

To detail what mathematical reasoning and sense making should look like across the high school curriculum, *Focus in High School Mathematics: Reasoning and Sense Making* offers a list of "reasoning habits." The intent here is not to present a new list of topics to be added to the high school curriculum: "Approaching the list as a new set of topics to be taught in an already crowded curriculum is not likely to have the desired effect. Instead, attention to reasoning habits needs to be integrated within the curriculum to ensure that students both understand and can use what they are taught" (NCTM 2009, p. 9). The reasoning habits are described and illustrated in the examples throughout the companion books in the Focus in High School Mathematics series.

Key Elements

Focus in High School Mathematics: Reasoning and Sense Making identifies "key elements" for each strand. These key elements are intended to furnish "a lens through which to view the potential of high school programs for promoting mathematical reasoning and sense making" (NCTM 2009, p. 18).

Content Expectations

As *Focus in High School Mathematics: Reasoning and Sense Making* suggests, readers wishing for more detailed content recommendations should refer to chapter 7, "Standards for Grades 9–12," in *Principles and Standards for School Mathematics* (NCTM 2000). However, for the readers' convenience, the appendix of each volume shows the relevant Principles or Standards for students in grades 9–12.

Introduction to *Focus in High School Mathematics: Fostering Reasoning and Sense Making for All Students*

Excellence in mathematics education rests on equity—high expectations, respect, understanding, and strong support for all students. Policies, practices, attitudes, and beliefs related to mathematics teaching and learning must be assessed continually to ensure that all students have equal access to the resources with the greatest potential to promote learning. A culture of equity maximizes the learning potential of all students. . . . Different solutions, interpretations, and approaches that are mathematically sound must be celebrated and integrated into class deliberations about problems. All members of the classroom group must accept the responsibility to engage with and support one another throughout the learning experience.

—NCTM Position Statement on Equity (2008)

Focus in High School Mathematics: Fostering Reasoning and Sense Making for All Students is a volume in a series of books that expand on the vision of *Focus in High School Mathematics: Reasoning and Sense Making*. Its focus is the crucial issue of making reasoning and sense making an important part of the daily mathematical experience of all high school students no matter what mathematics class they are taking. "All high school students" includes low-performing students; gifted students; students of different racial, sociolinguistic, and socioeconomic status; students with disabilities; and students who are mathematically talented—both those who are interested in taking the traditional fourth-year calculus course and those who are not.

The first chapter focuses on mathematical classroom experiences that lead to students' developing reasoning and sense-making skills that last beyond their formal schooling. Boaler discusses two studies that showed that pedagogy matters. She explains how teachers made reasoning and sense making a core part of their practice at Railside High and how that changed the students they taught—not only in their achievement but also in how they valued other people and how they saw the world. In the second study she describes two UK schools. She followed students through their math classes for three years and then followed up with them some eight years later to find out how their teachers' emphasis on reasoning and sense making had affected the students' lives.

Moschkovich begins chapter 2 with the assumption that language is not "the problem" for students who are learning English. Although the chapter does not present simple recipes for teaching English language learners or offer a quick fix, we hope that the recommendations will help to guide teachers in developing their own approaches to supporting mathematical reasoning and sense making for students who are learning English.

In chapter 3, Dieker and colleagues took on the challenge of focusing the broad topic of addressing the needs of all students with disabilities in mathematics. Since special educators have specialty areas that cover mild disabilities; moderate disabilities; severe profound disabilities; visual impairments; hearing impairments; physical disabilities; and behavioral challenges at the elementary, middle, or high school level, one chapter cannot cover all possible types of disabilities. However, the authors have developed a strong overview that will help those involved with secondary mathematics to make sense of and reason about why and how students with disabilities need to be a part of efforts to reform high school mathematics. Their attempt throughout the chapter is twofold: (1) to discuss the potential for students with disabilities and the presence of special education professionals in classrooms focused on reasoning and sense making (as the literature defines these concepts) and (2) to offer some practical foundational examples regarding how to address the range of disabilities that a high school teacher might encounter in today's classroom relative to the research base.

Every high school has gifted students, though the traditional methods and standardized tests might not identify them as such. In chapter 4, Teague and colleagues claim that without the proper motivation, encouragement, and intellectual challenge, we may lose some gifted students' mathematical talents forever. Thus, the authors propose strategies for working with gifted and talented students in the regular mathematics classroom as well as in advanced-placement courses.

According to Stiff and Johnson in chapter 5, rejecting what is easy and doing what is right takes leadership. This chapter challenges schools to use data to move students forward instead of denying them access to important mathematics. The authors show how at-risk models have promoted low expectations and how implementing pro-equity models can increase the mathematical opportunities of all students, thereby closing service, achievement, and opportunity gaps.

In chapter 6, Strutchens, Quander, and Gutiérrez show how strong mathematics learning communities can foster all students' reaching their full mathematics potential. This chapter uses examples from the research to show how constituents—including mathematics teachers, principals, students, and parents—have come together in schools to effect positive changes in students' mathematics learning.

We hope that these chapters will help further the dialogue about how to create for all students empowering mathematical experiences that incorporate reasoning and sense making. We also hope that focusing on particular aspects of the challenge will help to move the discourse beyond general statements—which may be easy to support but difficult to understand how to enact—to more specific consideration of how to achieve the vision of *Focus in High School Mathematics: Reasoning and Sense Making* for all students.

References

National Council of Teachers of Mathematics (NCTM). *Curriculum and Evaluation Standards for School Mathematics.* Reston, Va.: NCTM, 1989.

———. *Principles and Standards for School Mathematics.* Reston, Va.: NCTM, 2000.

———. *Curriculum Focal Points for Prekindergarten through Grade 8 Mathematics: A Quest for Coherence.* Reston, Va.: NCTM, 2006.

———. *Mathematics Teaching Today: Improving Practice, Improving Student Learning.* 2nd ed. Reston, Va.: NCTM, 2007.

———. "Equity in Mathematics Education." January 2008. www.nctm.org/about/content.aspx?id=13490 (accessed September 12, 2010).

———. *Focus in High School Mathematics: Reasoning and Sense Making.* Reston, Va.: NCTM, 2009.

Chapter 1

Stories of Success: Changing Students' Lives through Sense Making and Reasoning

Jo Boaler

Over my years of researching mathematics classrooms in England and the United States, I have been fortunate enough to study two examples of secondary math teachers' bringing about incredible and exciting achievements for students. Both teachers focused on reasoning and sense making, and I will describe how their actions in classrooms led students to great success not only in school but also in the rest of their lives. Often researchers measure the success of different approaches by focusing on test scores. I will share the test scores of students taught in different ways, but I will also show that students' experiences in math classrooms that focused on sense making had an impact far beyond test performance. This is because learning is an experience that changes us as people; learning is not merely accumulating facts and information but also a way of shaping our beliefs, ideas, and lives. For the U.S. study, for which I followed students through four years of math classes, I will explain how teachers made reasoning and sense making a core part of their practice and how that changed their students—not only in achievement but also in how they valued other people and how they saw the world. For the UK study, I followed students through their math classes for three years and then followed up with them some eight years later to find out how their teachers' emphasis on reasoning and sense making had affected their lives. We will learn about students from a wide range of backgrounds who came to love math, to achieve at high levels, and to have a different life because of their math classrooms.

The Communicative Approach

Railside High School is an urban California high school with students from many cultures and ethnicities. The sound of speeding trains often interrupts lessons. As with many urban schools, the buildings look as though they need some repair. But Railside is not like other urban schools in all respects. Calculus classes in urban schools often have poor enrollment or are nonexistent, but at Railside, eager and successful students pack these classes. Visitors to the math classrooms were amazed, seeing all the students hard at work, engaged, and excited about math. For a research project I conducted at Stanford University, we compared the learning of the Railside students to that of a similar-sized group of students in two other high schools offering mathematics through a more typical, traditional approach. In the traditional classes the students sat in rows at individual desks; they did not talk about mathematics or engage in sense making or reasoning. Instead the students watched the teacher demonstrate procedures at the start of lessons and then worked through textbooks filled with short, procedural questions. The two schools using the traditional approach were more suburban, and students started the schools with higher mathematics achievement levels than those of the students at Railside. But by the end of the first year of our research study, the Railside students were achieving at the same levels as the students in the more suburban schools on tests of algebra; by the end of the second year, the Railside

students were significantly outperforming the other students on tests of algebra and geometry (Boaler and Staples 2008; Boaler 2008a).

In addition to the high achievement at Railside, the students enjoyed math more. In surveys administered at various times during the four years of the study, the students at Railside were always significantly more positive and more interested in mathematics than the students from the other classes. By their senior year, an incredible 41 percent of the Railside seniors were in advanced classes of precalculus and calculus, compared with only 23 percent of students from traditional classes. Further, when we interviewed 105 students (mainly seniors) at the end of the study about their future plans, almost all students from the traditional classes said that they had decided not to further pursue mathematics as a subject—even when they had succeeded. Only 5 percent of students from the traditional classes planned a future in mathematics, compared with 39 percent of Railside students. Perhaps most impressive of all: when students had started Railside, different ethnic and cultural groups had significant achievement differences, but by the time they left Railside all the differences had diminished and sometimes disappeared. The achievement differences between students of different ethnic and cultural groups remained in the other schools that taught mathematics traditionally.

I first visited Railside in 1999 because I had learned that the teachers collaborated and planned teaching ideas together, and I was interested to see their lessons. I saw enough in that visit to invite the school to be part of a new project to investigate the effectiveness of different mathematics approaches. Some four years later, after a team of doctoral students from Stanford University and I had observed, interviewed, and assessed 700 students as they progressed through different high schools, we knew that Railside's approach was both highly successful and highly unusual.

The mathematics teachers at Railside used to teach by using traditional methods, but the teachers were unhappy with the high failure rates among students and the students' lack of interest in math, so the teachers worked together to design a new approach. Teachers met together over several summers to devise a new algebra curriculum and later to improve all the courses offered. They also detracked classes and made algebra the first course that all students would take upon entering high school. In most algebra classes, students work through questions designed to give practice on mathematical techniques such as factoring polynomials or solving inequalities. At Railside the students learned the same methods, but the curriculum was organized around bigger mathematical ideas, with unifying themes such as "What is a linear function?" A focus of the Railside approach was multiple representations, which is why I have described it as communicative—the students learned about the different ways that mathematics could be communicated through words, diagrams, tables, symbols, objects, and graphs. As the students worked in their groups, they were always asked to explain work to each other, moving between different representations and communicative forms. Students worked in groups all the time, and the problems they worked on were longer and more conceptual than those the students in the traditional schools worked on (I give an example later). As the students worked in their groups, they were asked to explain their reasoning to each other and to the teacher. The students were taught to be responsible for each other's learning, and they were allowed to move on to a new problem only when everyone in the group had understood. In support of this approach, students at Railside were taught that they had two important responsibilities in math class: to ask for help if they needed it and to help anyone who needed it. After the groups had worked for a while, the teachers asked different students to come and present ideas to the class—to reason and to make sense of their methods and solutions publicly—and teachers encouraged students to ask the presenters for reasons, as third-year students Latisha and Ana explained:

Interviewer: What happens when someone says an answer?

Ana: We'll ask how they got it.

Latisha: Yeah, because we do that a lot in class. . . . Some of the students—it'll be the students that don't do their work, that'd be the ones, they'll be the ones to ask step by step. But a lot of people would probably ask how to approach it. And then if they did something else, they would show how they did it. And then you just have a little session!

The Railside classrooms were all organized in groups, and students helped each other as they worked. The teachers paid attention to how the groups worked together, and they taught students to respect the contributions of other students, regardless of prior achievement or status.

One unfortunate but common effect in such situations is that sometimes students develop beliefs about the inferiority or superiority of different students. In the traditional classes we studied, students talked about other students as smart and dumb, quick and slow. At Railside, the students did not talk in these ways; they talked instead about students who did or did not do their work (as Latisha's preceding comment shows). This did not mean that they thought all students were the same, but they came to appreciate the diversity of the classes and the various attributes that different students offered. Zane, a second-year student, said, "Everybody in there is at a different level. But what makes the class good is that everybody's at different levels, so everybody's constantly teaching each other and helping each other out."

The teachers at Railside followed an approach called complex instruction, designed to make group work more effective and to promote equity in classrooms (Cohen and Lotan 1997). The teachers continually emphasized that all children were smart and had strengths in different areas and that everyone had something important to offer when working on math. One interesting aspect of the complex-instruction approach is the creation of multidimensional classrooms. Many mathematics classrooms value one practice above all others: executing procedures correctly and quickly. The narrowness by which this system judges success means that some students rise to the top of classes, gaining good grades and teacher praise, whereas others sink to the bottom—and most students know who falls into each category. Such classrooms are unidimensional: the dimensions along which success is presented are singular. At Railside the teachers created multidimensional classes by valuing many dimensions of mathematical work. They achieved this outcome in part by having students work in groups and by giving students "group-worthy problems": open-ended problems that illustrated important mathematical concepts, allowed for multiple representations, and focused on sense making and reasoning. But the school's approach had another, rarer important aspect: the teachers enacted an expanded conception of mathematics and "smartness." The teachers at Railside knew that being good at mathematics involves many different ways of working, as mathematicians' accounts tell us. It involves asking and making sense of questions, drawing pictures and graphs, rephrasing problems, and justifying and reasoning, in addition to calculating with procedures. Instead of just rewarding the correct use of procedures, Railside teachers encouraged and rewarded all these different ways of being mathematical.

In interviews with students from both the traditional and the Railside classes, we asked students what succeeding in math class took. Students from the traditional classes were unanimous: it involved paying careful attention—watching what the teacher did and then doing the same. Students from the Railside classes talked of many different activities, including asking good questions, re-phrasing problems, explaining ideas, being logical, justifying methods, representing ideas, and bring-ing a different perspective to a problem. Put simply: because Railside offered many more ways to succeed, many more students *did*. The following interview comments from Janet and Jasmine, both first-year students, indicate the multidimensionality of classes and the central role of reasoning and sense making.

Janet: Back in middle school, the only thing you worked on was your math skills. But here you work socially, and you also try to learn to help people and get help. Like, you im-prove on your social skills, math skills, and logic skills.

Jasmine: With math you have to interact with everybody and talk to them and answer their questions. You can't be just, like, "Oh, here's the book, look at the numbers and figure it out."

Interviewer: Why is that different for math?

Jasmine: It's not just one way to do it. . . . It's more interpretive. It's not just one answer. There's more than one way to get it. And then it's, like, "Why does it work?"

Hearing students describe mathematics as broader and more *interpretive* than other subjects is rare. This breadth and the teachers' continued emphasis on "why does it work?" were important to the high levels of success and participation.

The teachers also used roles in complex instruction. In groups, students had a particular role to play, such as facilitator, team captain, recorder/reporter, or resource manager (Cohen and Lotan 1997). Teachers gave students roles to ensure that everyone had something important to do and to make the group work more equal. Railside teachers often emphasized the different roles. For ex-ample, they would pause at the start of class to remind facilitators to help people check answers or explain their thinking or to ask the group "what did you get for number 1?" or "did anyone get a different answer?" Or they would ask recorder/reporters whether their group needed to go over any problem with the teacher. Students changed roles at the end of each unit of work, which usually took a few weeks. The roles contributed to the impressive ways that students interacted in the classrooms as they learned that everyone had something important to do and that all students could rely on each other. Railside teachers were also careful about identifying and talking to students about all the ways in which the students were smart. The teachers knew that students—and adults—were often severely hampered in their mathematical work by thinking that they were not smart enough. The teachers also knew that every student could contribute much to mathematics and so took it upon themselves to identify and encourage students' strengths. This approach paid off, and the motivated and eager students who believed in themselves and knew they could succeed in mathematics would have im-pressed any visitor to the school.

The Railside teachers brought about incredible achievements, including reductions in inequali-ties as evidenced by test scores, through the reasoning and justification that they required students to give. Linking the inherently mathematical practice of reasoning with the promotion of equity may seem odd, but at Railside we observed a direct link between the two, for these reasons: One of the most difficult challenges that any mathematics teacher faces is students' different levels of knowledge and understanding. At Railside the classes were heterogeneous, so different students' un-derstanding varied widely. But the fact that students were always taught to reason and justify helped with differences in student understanding: students who didn't understand work had extra opportuni-ties to hear explanations and justifications from other students and to understand their work. Latisha (quoted earlier) said, "it'll be the students that don't do their work, that'd be the ones, they'll be the ones to ask step by step," indicating some of the support that reasoning afforded struggling students.

The following extract comes from second-year student Juan, one of the lower-achieving students; his description of how he copied work from someone else indicates the support that the school's focus on sense making and reasoning conveyed: "Most of them, they just, like, know what to do and everything. First you're, like, 'Why you put this?' and then, like, if I do my work and compare it to theirs . . . theirs is, like, super different 'cause they know, like, what to do. I will be, like, 'Let me copy'; I will be, like, 'Why you did this?' And then I'd be, like, 'I don't get it why you got that.' And then, like, sometimes the answer's just, like, they be, like, 'Yeah, he's right and you're wrong.' But, like, why?"

Juan had learned that it was his right to ask why and to keep asking why until he understood, which led him to encourage the student from whom he was copying to reason and justify his thinking, giving Juan more access to understanding.

In the following I give an example of one classroom activity I observed and how that teacher worked with students to encourage sense making and reasoning in their learning of algebra.

Making algebra meaningful

In one lesson I observed, students were learning about functions. The students had been given what the teachers called "pile patterns." Different students received different patterns to work with. Pedro received the following pattern, which includes the first three cases:

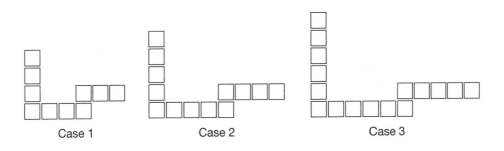

| Case 1 | Case 2 | Case 3 |

The activity was for students to work out how the pattern was growing and to represent this as an algebraic rule, a *t*-table, a graph, and a generic pattern; they also needed to show the 100th case in the sequence, having seen the first three cases.

Pedro started by working out the numbers for the first three cases, and he put these in his *t*-table:

Case number	Number of tiles
1	10
2	13
3	16

He noted at this point that the pattern was "growing" by 3 each time. Next he tried to see how the pattern was growing in his shapes, and after a few minutes he saw it. He could see that each section grew by 1 each time. He represented the first two cases in the following way:

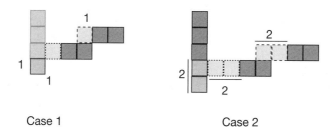

Case 1   Case 2

He could see that 7 tiles always stayed the same and were present in the same positions (this was how he visualized the pattern's growth, but other ways also exist). In addition to the "constant" 7, there were tiles that grew with every case number. So if we just look at the vertical line of tiles,

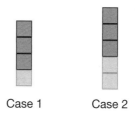

Case 1   Case 2

we see case 1 has 1 at the bottom, plus 3. Case 2 has 2 plus 3. Case 3 would have 3 plus 3, and case 4 would have 4 plus 3, and so on. The 3 is a constant, but each time one more is added to the lower section of tiles. We can also see that the growing section is the same size as the case number each time. When the case is 1, the total number of tiles is 1 plus 3; when the case is 2, the total is 2 plus 3; we can assume from this pattern that in the 100th case, we will get 100 + 3 tiles. This sort of work—considering, visualizing, and describing patterns—is at the heart of mathematics and its applications. Pedro represented his pattern algebraically in the following way:

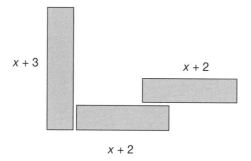

$x + 3$ $x + 2$

$x + 2$

Here x stood for the case number. By adding together the three sections, he could now represent the whole function as $3x + 7$.

Mathematicians, scientists, medics, computer programmers, and many other professionals use algebra so pervasively because it is a key method in describing patterns, which grow and change and are central to their work and to the world. The task in this problem—finding a way of visualizing, representing, and making sense of the pattern and using algebra to describe its changing parts—is important algebraic work.

Pedro was pleased with his work, and he decided to check his algebraic expression with his *t*-table. Satisfied that $3x + 7$ worked, he set about plotting his values on a graph. I left the group as he was eagerly reaching for graph paper and colored pencils. The next day in class I checked with him again. He was sitting with three other boys, and they were designing a poster to show their four functions. Their four desks were pushed together and covered by a large poster divided into four sections. From a distance the poster looked like a piece of mathematical artwork with color-coded diagrams, arrows connecting different representations, and large algebraic symbols.

After a while the teacher came over and looked at the boys' work, talking with them about their diagrams, graphs, and algebraic expressions; probing their thinking; and encouraging them to make sense of their work. The teacher asked Pedro where his graph represented the 7 (from $3x + 7$). Pedro showed the teacher and then decided to show the +7 in the same color on his tile patterns, on his graph, and in his algebraic expression. Communicating key features of functions by using color coding was something that all Railside students learned, to give meaning to the different representations. This technique helped the students learn something important: the algebraic expression represents something tangible, and one can see the relationships within the expression in the tables, graphs, and diagrams. This approach was one way that the teachers encouraged reasoning and sense making through algebraic work.

As well as producing posters that showed linear and nonlinear patterns, the students were asked to find and connect patterns—both in their own pile patterns and across all four teammates' patterns—and to show the patterns by using technical writing tools. One aim of the lesson was to teach students to look for patterns within and among representations and to begin to understand generalization.

The tasks at Railside were designed to be open enough to be thought about in different ways, and they often required that students show their thinking by using different mathematical representations and make sense of what they were doing, reasoning about their different decisions.

Relational equity

It would be hard to spend years in the classrooms at Railside without noticing that the students were not just learning mathematics effectively but were also learning to treat each other more respectfully than is typical in schools. The students told us in interviews that they did not have ethnic cliques in their school because of the approach used in math classes (which other subject lessons did not, at the time, use). I have described the approach of the Railside teachers as equitable partly because students achieved more equitable outcomes on tests, but the students at Railside also learned to act more equitably in their classrooms. Students learned to appreciate the contributions of students from many different cultural groups and with many different characteristics and perspectives. Researchers considering equity usually look for differences in test scores between students of different groups. Such differences are important, but when I studied the Railside classrooms I began to ask myself: Can we teach math in ways that encourage equitable relations between students? Can students be taught ways of working and ways of regarding each other that are more equitable, with students valuing each other despite any differences in achievement, social class, gender, or race? The Railside teachers managed to achieve such equitable relations between students (see also Boaler [2008a]).

Many believe that students learn respect for different people and cultures if they discuss such issues or read diverse forms of literature in English or social studies classes. I propose that all subjects have something to contribute in promoting equity—including mathematics, which people often regard as the most abstract subject, removed from responsibilities of cultural or social awareness. At Railside the respectful relationships that students developed across cultures and genders, and that they took into their lives beyond school, were made possible by a mathematics approach that was mainly abstract but that valued different insights, methods, and sense making in the collective solving of particular problems. That students were asked to make sense of problems and that different students would see the problems in different ways, which teachers praised and valued, meant that students started to value other people's thinking more broadly. This valuation was particularly important in classrooms that were multiracial and multilingual. Tanita and Carol, both fourth-year students, give a sense of how the classroom's focus on sense making and reasoning led to their developing open minds and to valuing the contributions of different students:

Tanita: You got everyone's perspective on it, 'cause, like, when you're debating it, a rule or a method, you get someone else's perspective of what they think instead of just going off your own thoughts. That's why it was good with, like, a lot of people.

Carol: I liked it, too. Most people opened up their ideas.

Ayana, also a fourth-year student, told us why she appreciated considering different methods in mathematics class:

Ayana: I think it helps, because it helps with learning to get out of your comfort zone, 'cause whenever you learn, you're not always going to learn the exact way, so to be able to learn different types of ways, if someone interprets something the way they do, and then you look at it and you're like, "Oh, look at this," and you see it their ways, you never know later on when you might have to change your interpretation or something. So it allows you to come out of, like, your comfort zone.

In different research studies in England and the United States, I interviewed hundreds of students who have worked in groups (Boaler 2008a). Virtually all students reported that they prefer working in groups to working alone, but students generally list benefits that are exclusively about their own learning. At Railside, students' descriptions were distinctly reciprocal as they voiced a clear concern for the learning of their classmates as well as their own learning. First-year student Amado reflected this sentiment:

Interviewer: Do you prefer to work alone or in groups?

Amado: I think it'd be in groups, 'cause I want, like, people that doesn't know how to understand it, I want to help them. And I want to . . . I want them to be good at it. And I want them to understand how to do the math that we do.

Students also talked about their enjoyment of helping others and the value in helping each other; Latisha is one example:

Latisha: It's good working in groups because everybody else in the group can learn with you, so if someone doesn't understand—like, if I don't understand but the other person does understand—they can explain it to me, or vice versa, and I think it's cool.

At Railside the students enjoyed math and achieved highly; both results came about through an approach that was based on collective, rather than individual, work; responsibility toward other students; and a constant encouragement to make sense of work, by themselves and with others. In addition to these impressive achievements, the Railside students learned to work equitably—to listen to and give regard to other students' ideas and to treat each other with respect—something that went well beyond their mathematics achievement.

The Project-Based Approach

In this section we will learn about how UK math teachers changed students' lives and opportunities many years after math classes had ended.

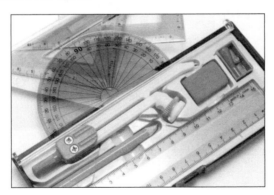

Phoenix Park School

The day that I walked into Phoenix Park School, in a working-class area of England, I didn't know what to expect. I had invited the math department at the school to be a part of my research project. I knew that the department used a project-based approach, but I did not know much more than that. I made my way across the playground and into the school buildings on that first morning with some trepidation. A group of students congregated outside their math classroom at break time, and I asked them what I should expect from the lesson I was about to see. "Chaos," said one of the students;

"freedom," said another. Their descriptions were curious and made me more excited to see the lesson. Some three years later, after moving with the students through school, observing hundreds of lessons, and researching the students' learning, I knew exactly what they meant.

This was to be my first longitudinal research project on different ways of learning mathematics and, as with the Railside study, I watched hundreds of hours of lessons, interviewed and gave surveys to students, and performed various assessments. I chose to follow an entire cohort of students in two schools, from when they were 13 to when they were 16 years of age. One school, Phoenix Park, used a project-based approach; the other, Amber Hill, used the more typical, traditional approach. I chose the two schools not only because of their different approaches but also because the student intakes were demographically similar, the teachers were well qualified, and the students had followed the same mathematics approaches up to the age of 13, when my research began. At that time, the students at the two schools scored at the same levels on national mathematics tests; then their mathematical pathways diverged.

The classrooms at Phoenix Park did look chaotic. The project-based approach meant a lot less order and control than in traditional approaches. Instead of teaching procedures that students would practice, the teachers gave the students projects to work on that *needed* mathematical methods. From the beginning of year 8 (when students started at the school) to three-quarters of the way through year 10, the students worked on open-ended projects in every lesson. The students didn't learn separate areas of mathematics, such as algebra or geometry, because English schools do not separate mathematics in that way; instead, the students learned "maths," the whole subject, every year. The students were taught in mixed-ability groups, and projects usually lasted for about three weeks.

At the start of the different projects, the teachers introduced students to a problem or a theme that the students explored, using their own ideas and the mathematical methods that they were learning. The problems usually had an open format so that students could take the work in directions of interest to them. For example, in the Volume 216 problem, the students were simply told that the volume of an object was 216, and they were asked to go away and think about what the object could be, what dimensions it would have, and what it would look like. Sometimes teachers taught the students mathematical content that could be useful to them before they started a new project. More typically, though, the teachers introduced methods to individuals or small groups when they encountered a need for them in the particular project they were working on. Simon and Philip, year 10 students, described the school's math approach in this way:

Simon: We're usually set a task first and we're taught the skills needed to do the task, and then we get on with the task, and we ask the teacher for help.

Philip: Or you're just set the task and then you go about it in . . . you explore the different things, and they help you in doing that . . . so you sort of . . . so different skills are sort of tailored to different tasks.

Interviewer: And do you all do the same thing?

Philip: You're all given the same task, but how you go about it, how you do it and what level you do it at . . . changes, doesn't it?

The students were given an unusual degree of freedom in math lessons. They were usually given choices between different projects to work on, and they were encouraged to decide the nature and direction of their work. Sometimes the different projects varied in difficulty, and the teachers guided students toward projects that they thought were suited to students' strengths. During one of my visits to the classrooms, students were working on a project called 36 Fences. The teacher started the project by asking all the students to gather around the board at the front of the room. Chairs shuffled as students made their way to the front, sitting in an arc around the board. Jim, the teacher, explained that a farmer had 36 individual fences, each 1 meter long, and that he wanted to put them together to make the biggest possible area. Jim then asked students what shapes they thought the fences could be arranged into. Students suggested a rectangle, triangle, or square. "How about a pentagon?" Jim asked. The students thought about this and talked about it. Jim asked them whether they wanted to make irregular shapes allowable.

After some discussion, Jim asked the students to go back to their desks and think about the biggest possible area that the fences could make. Students at Phoenix Park were allowed to choose whom they worked with, and some of them left the discussion to work alone, whereas most worked in pairs or groups. Some students began by investigating different sizes of rectangles and squares; others plotted graphs to investigate how areas changed with different side lengths. The students at Phoenix Park were encouraged to use math to make sense of the situations they were given, and the teachers gave constant encouragement to explain why methods worked, justifying and reasoning as they worked.

Susan was working alone, investigating hexagons, and she explained to me that she was working out the area of a regular hexagon by dividing it into six triangles, and she had drawn one of the triangles separately. She explained that she knew that the angle at the top of each triangle must be 60 degrees, so she could draw the triangles exactly to scale by using compasses and find the area by measuring the height.

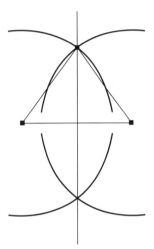

I left Susan working and moved to sit with a table of boys. Mickey had found that the biggest area for a rectangle with perimeter 36 is 9 × 9—this gave him the idea that shapes with equal sides may give bigger areas, and he started to think about equilateral triangles. Mickey seemed interested by his work, and he was about to draw an equilateral triangle when he was distracted by Ahmed, who told him to forget triangles. Ahmed had found that the shape with the largest area made of 36 fences was a 36-sided shape. Ahmed told Mickey to find the area of a 36-sided shape too, and Ahmed leaned across the table excitedly, explaining how to do this. He explained that you divide the 36-sided shape into triangles and all the triangles must have a 1-cm base. Mickey joined in, saying, "Yes, and their angles must be 10 degrees!" Ahmed said, "Yes, but you have to find the height, and to do that you need the "tan" button on your calculator, T-A-N. I'll show you how; Mr. Collins has just shown me."

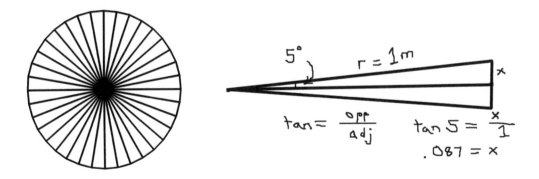

Mickey and Ahmed moved closer together, using the tangent ratio to calculate the area. As the class worked on their investigations of the 36 Fences problem, many students divided shapes into triangles, giving the teacher the opportunity to introduce trigonometric ratios. The students were excited to learn about trig ratios: trig ratios enabled the students to go further in their investigations, the ratios made sense to them in the context of a real problem, and the methods were useful. In later activities, the students revisited their knowledge of trig ratios and used them to solve other problems.

At Phoenix Park, the teachers taught mathematical methods to help students solve problems and make sense of the world around them. Students learned about statistics and probability, for example, as they worked on a set of activities called Interpreting the World. During that project they interpreted data on college attendance, pregnancies, football results, and other issues of interest to them. Students learned aspects of algebra as they investigated different patterns and represented them symbolically; they learned about trigonometry through a series of projects such as the 36 Fences projects and by investigating the shadows of objects. The teachers carefully chose the different projects to interest the students and to create opportunities for learning important and meaningful mathematical concepts and methods. Some projects were applied, requiring that students engage with real-world situations; other activities started with a context, such as 36 Fences, but led into abstract investigations. As students worked, they learned new methods, they chose methods they knew, and they adapted and applied both. Not surprisingly, the Phoenix Park students came to view mathematical methods as flexible problem-solving tools. When I interviewed Lindsey, a second-year student, she described the mathematics approach, saying, "Well, if you find a rule or a method, you try and adapt it to other things. When we found this rule that worked with the circles, we started to work out the percentages and then adapted it, so we just took it further and took different steps and tried to adapt it to new situations."

Students had many choices as they worked. They were allowed to choose whether they worked in groups, in pairs, or alone. They were often given choices about activities to work on, and they were always encouraged to take problems in directions that were of interest to them and to work at appropriate levels. Most of the students liked this mathematical freedom, as Simon told me: "You're able to explore; there's not many limits, and that's more interesting." Discipline was relaxed at Phoenix Park, and students also had a lot of freedom to work or not work.

Amber Hill School

At Amber Hill School, the teachers used the traditional approach that is common in England and in the United States. The teachers began lessons by lecturing from the board, introducing students to mathematical methods; students then worked through exercises in their books. When the students at Amber Hill learned trigonometry, they were not introduced to it as a way of solving problems; instead, they were told to remember the following:

$$\text{"SOH"} \quad \sin \theta = \frac{O}{H}$$

$$\text{"CAH"} \quad \cos \theta = \frac{A}{H}$$

$$\text{"TOA"} \quad \tan \theta = \frac{O}{A}$$

H = Hypotenuse

O = Opposite

A = Adjacent

And they practiced by working through many short questions. The exercises at Amber Hill typically consisted of short, contextualized mathematics questions, such as this one: *Helen rides a bike for 1 hour at 30 km/h and 2 hours at 15 km/h. What is Helen's average speed for the journey?*

Classrooms were peaceful and quiet at Amber Hill, and students worked quietly, on task, for almost all their lessons. Students always sat in pairs, and they were generally allowed to converse quietly—usually checking answers with each other but not encouraged to have mathematical discussions. During the three years that I observed the students as they progressed through school, I learned that they worked hard but that most disliked mathematics. The students at Amber Hill came to believe that mathematics was a subject that involved only memorizing rules and procedures, as Stephen described to me: "In maths, there's a certain formula to get to, say, from *a* to *b*, and there's no other way to get to it, or maybe there is, but you've got to remember the formula, you've got to remember it." More worryingly, the students at Amber Hill became so convinced of the need to memorize the methods they were shown that many of them saw no place for thought, as Louise, a student in the highest group, told me: "In maths you have to remember; in other subjects, you can think about it."

Amber Hill's approach stood in stark contrast to Phoenix Park's: the Amber Hill students spent more time on task, but they thought mathematics was a set of rules that needed to be memorized, and few of them developed the levels of interest that the Phoenix Park students developed. In lessons the Amber Hill students were often successful, getting many questions right in their exercises, but they often got them right by following cues, not by understanding the mathematical ideas or making sense of the questions. For example, the biggest cue telling students how to answer a question was the method they had just had explained on the board. The students knew that if they used the method they had just been shown, they were probably going to get the questions right. They also knew that when they moved from exercise A to exercise B, they should do something slightly more complicated. They also followed other cues: they knew that they should use all the lines given to them in a diagram and all the numbers in a question; if they didn't use them all, they thought they were doing something wrong. Unfortunately, the same cues were not present in the exams, as Gary told me, when describing why he found the exams hard: "It's different, and, like, the way it's there, like, is not the same. It doesn't, like, tell you it, the story, the question; it's not the same as in the books, the way the teacher works it out." Gary seemed to be suggesting, as I had seen in my observations, that he didn't try to make sense of problems because the story or the question in their books often gave away what they had to do, but the exam questions didn't. Trevor also talked about cues when he explained why his exam grade hadn't been good: "You can get a trigger, when she says, like, 'simultaneous equations' and 'graphs' or 'graphically.' When they say, like, and you know, it pushes that trigger, tells you what to do." I asked him, "What happens in the exam when you haven't got that?" He gave a clear answer: "You panic."

In England all students take the same national examination in mathematics at age 16. The examination is a three-hour, traditional test made up of short mathematics questions. Despite the difference in the two school approaches, the students' preparation for the examination was fairly similar: both schools gave students old exams to work through and practice. At Phoenix Park the teachers stopped the project work a few weeks before the examination and focused on teaching any standard methods that students may not have met. They spent more time lecturing from the board, and classrooms looked similar (briefly) to those at Amber Hill.

Many people expected the Amber Hill students to do well on the examinations, since their approach was meant to be examination oriented, but the Phoenix Park students attained significantly higher examination grades. The Phoenix Park students also achieved higher grades than the national average, despite having started their school at levels significantly lower than the national average.

The Amber Hill students faced many problems in the examination, which they were not expecting since they had worked so hard in lessons. In class, the Amber Hill students had always been shown methods and then practiced them. In the examination they needed to choose methods to use, and many of them found that difficult. As Alan explained to me, "It's stupid, really, 'cause when you're in the lesson, when you're doing work—even when it's hard—you get the odd one or two wrong, but most of them you get right, and you think, 'Well, when I go into the exam I'm gonna get most of them right,' 'cause you get all your chapters right. But you don't." Even when it was obvious which methods to use for the examination questions, the Amber Hill students would often confuse the steps they had learned because they had never been encouraged to make sense of their work. For example, when the Amber Hill students answered a question on simultaneous equations, they attempted to use the standard procedure they had been taught, but only 26 percent of students used the procedure correctly. The rest of the students used a confused and jumbled version of the procedure and received no credit for the question.

The Phoenix Park students had not met all the methods they needed in the examination, but they had been taught to solve problems and to make sense of situations, and they approached the examination questions in the same flexible way as they approached their projects: choosing, adapting, and applying the methods they had learned. I asked Angus whether he thought the exam included things that they hadn't seen before. He thought for a while and said, "Well, sometimes, I suppose, they put it in a way which throws you, but if there's stuff I actually haven't done before, I'll try and make as much sense of it as I can, try and understand it and answer it as best as I can, and if it's wrong, it's wrong."

The Phoenix Park students didn't do better only on the examinations. For part of my research, I investigated the usefulness of the approach to students' lives. One way I measured this over the three years was by giving students a range of assessments designed to assess use of mathematics in real-world situations. In the architectural activity, for example, students had to measure a model house, use a scale plan, estimate, and decide on appropriate house dimensions. The Phoenix Park students outperformed the Amber Hill students on all the assessments. By the time I was completing the research, most students had jobs that they undertook in the evenings and on weekends. When I interviewed the students at both schools about their use of mathematics outside school, stark differences emerged. All forty Amber Hill students that I interviewed said that they would never use their school-learned methods in any situation outside school, as Richard told me: "Well, when I'm out of school, the maths from here is nothing to do with it, to tell you the truth. . . . Most of the things we've learned in school, we would never use anywhere." The Amber Hill students thought school mathematics was a strange sort of code that you would use in one place, the mathematics classroom, and they developed the idea that their school mathematics knowledge had boundaries or barriers surrounding it that kept it firmly within the mathematics classroom.

At Phoenix Park, the students were confident that they would use the methods they learned in school, and they could give me examples of their use of school-learned mathematics in their jobs and lives. Indeed, many students' descriptions suggested that they had learned mathematics in a way that transcended the boundaries that generally exist between the classroom and real situations.

Mathematics for life

Some years later, I caught up with the ex-students from Amber Hill and Phoenix Park, when they were about 24 years old, and talked to them about the usefulness of the mathematics teaching they had experienced. I had often been asked about the future of the students after they had left their schools, and so I decided to find out. I sent surveys to the ex-students' addresses and followed up the surveys with interviews. For part of the survey I asked the young people what jobs they were doing. I then classified all the jobs and put them onto a scale of social class, which indicated the professionalism of their jobs and the salaries they would have received. Doing so showed something interesting. When the students were in school, their social class levels (determined from parents' jobs) had been equal. Eight years after my study, the Phoenix Park young adults were working in more highly skilled and professional jobs than the Amber Hill adults, even though the survey respondents' school achievement range had been equal. Sixty-five percent of the Phoenix Park adults had moved into jobs that were more professional than those of their parents, compared with 23 percent of Amber Hill adults. Fifty-two percent of the Amber Hill adults were in less professional jobs than those of their parents, compared with only 15 percent of the Phoenix Park adults. At Phoenix Park a distinct upward trend in careers and economic well-being was evident; at Amber Hill there was not, even though Phoenix Park was in a less prosperous area.

In addition to the survey, I traveled back to England to conduct follow-up interviews. I contacted a representative group from each school, choosing young adults with comparable examination grades. In interviews, the Phoenix Park adults communicated a positive approach to work and life, describing how they used the sense-making approach they had experienced in their mathematics classrooms to solve problems and make sense of mathematical situations in their lives. Adrian had attended a university and studied economics, and he told me that "You often get lots of stuff where there will be graphs of economic situations in countries and stuff like that. And I would always look at those very critically. And I think the maths that I've learned is very useful for being able to actually see exactly how it's being presented, or whether it's being biased." When I asked Paul, a senior regional hotel manager, whether he found the mathematics that he had learned in school useful, he said that he did, telling me, "I suppose there was a lot of things I can relate back to maths in school. You know, it's about having a sort of concept, isn't it, of space and numbers and how you can relate that back. And then, okay, if you've got an idea about something and how you would then use maths to work that out . . . I suppose maths is about problem solving for me. It's about numbers, it's about problem solving, it's about being logical."

Whereas the Phoenix Park young adults talked of maths as a problem-solving tool, and they were generally positive about their school's approach, the Amber Hill students could not understand why their school's mathematics approach had prepared them so badly for the demands of the workplace. Bridget spoke sadly when she said, "It was never related to real life, I don't feel. I don't feel it was. And I think it would have been a lot better if I could have seen what I could use this stuff for, and just basically . . . because then it helps you to know *why*. You learn *why* that is that and *why* it ends up at that. And I think definitely relating it to real life is important." Bridget wanted an approach to maths that related to her life; she also highlighted the importance of knowing *why*.

Marcos was also puzzled why the school's maths approach had seemed so removed from the students' lives and work:

> It was something where you had to just remember in which order you did things, and that's it. It had no significance to me past that point at all—which is a shame. Because when you have parents like mine who keep on about maths and how important it is, and having that experience where it just seems to be not important to anything at all really. It was very abstract. And it was kind of almost purely theoretical. As with most things that are purely theoretical, without having some kind of association with anything tangible, you kind of forget it all.

Conclusion

The two successful teaching approaches I reviewed were the subject of comprehensive research studies. Although they were conducted in different countries, the findings pointed to the same conclusion: students need to be actively involved in their learning, and they need to be engaged in a broad form of mathematics, representing and communicating ideas, justifying methods and solutions, and making sense of their work. Much evidence indicates that, if students are encouraged to work in such ways, they will achieve more highly and they will enjoy math more (Boaler 2008a, 2008b; Schoenfeld 2002; Riordan and Noyce 2001; Maher 1991). But the two schools I was fortunate enough to study have shown two other important outcomes. For it seems that when students are encouraged to make sense of work, they can also learn to value different students' ideas and to respect each other—at the same time being better prepared to face the complex problem-solving demands of the workplace and their lives. Moving from a procedural to a sense-making approach in mathematics is not straightforward for teachers; it takes commitment, training, and time. But the outcomes of students at Phoenix Park and Railside suggest that such changes, no matter how hard they may be, are worthwhile in giving students a different and more positive start to their adult lives.

References

Boaler, Jo. *What's Math Got to Do with It? Helping Children Learn to Love Their Least Favorite Subject—and Why It's Important for America.* New York: Penguin, 2008a.

———. "Promoting 'Relational Equity' and High Mathematics Achievement through an Innovative Mixed Ability Approach." *British Educational Research Journal* 34, no. 2 (2008b): 167–94.

Boaler, Jo, and Megan Staples. "Creating Mathematical Futures through an Equitable Teaching Approach: The Case of Railside School." *Teachers College Record* 110 (January 2008): 608–45.

Cohen, Elizabeth, and Rachel Lotan, eds. *Working for Equity in Heterogeneous Classrooms: Sociological Theory in Practice.* New York: Teachers College Press, 1997.

Maher, Carolyn. "Is Dealing with Mathematics as a Thoughtful Subject Compatible with Maintaining Satisfactory Test Scores? A Nine-Year Study." *Journal of Mathematical Behavior* 10 (December 1991): 225–48.

Riordan, Julie E., and Pendred E. Noyce. "The Impact of Two Standards-Based Mathematics Curricula on Student Achievement in Massachusetts." *Journal for Research in Mathematics Education* 32 (July 2001): 368–98.

Schoenfeld, Alan H. "Making Mathematics Work for All Children: Issues of Standards, Testing, and Equity." *Educational Researcher* 31 (January–February 2002): 13–25.

Chapter 2

Supporting Mathematical Reasoning and Sense Making for English Learners

Judit N. Moschkovich

English learners are a large and growing population in U.S. schools. In 2001, 4.5 million K–12 students in public schools (9.3 percent) were labeled as English learners (Tafoya 2002). Between 1979 and 2006, the number of school-aged children (aged 5–17 years) in the population who spoke a language other than English at home more than doubled, increasing from 3.8 million (9 percent) to 10.8 million (20 percent) (Planty et al. 2008). Most English learners in the United States are Latinos/ Latinas. In 2006, about 72 percent of school-aged children who spoke a language other than English at home spoke Spanish (Planty et al. 2008). In some states the numbers are even greater. For example, in California, 25 percent (1.5 million) of the children in public school in 2001 were labeled English learners, and 83 percent of those children spoke Spanish as their primary language (Tafoya 2002).

As the population of English learners increases in U.S. public schools, so do concerns with the needs of these students in mathematics classrooms. Although language issues are important to consider in all mathematics classrooms, we seem most concerned with issues of language as they arise in classrooms with students who are learning English as a second language. Perhaps language issues seem more salient when the teacher and students obviously do not share a common language for instruction. However, as many mathematics teachers know, English learners and native speakers share some of the same challenges. For example, many students who are native English speakers have trouble understanding and solving word problems. We also know that students who are native English speakers may use words with meanings that differ from the mathematical meanings of words in a textbook. A native English speaker might respond to the question "Is a square a rectangle?" by saying "No, it's not," because the student is not using the mathematical meaning of the word *square*.

We could imagine that the solution to the problem of mathematics instruction for English learners involves a quick fix: new manuals for teachers, a new piece of software, a new teaching method, and so on. Unfortunately, such solutions risk reinforcing myths about language, how we learn a second language, and how we learn mathematics. This chapter's goal is to suggest recommendations for teaching practices that are based on research rather than on myths. A commitment to improving mathematics learning for all students—and especially for students who are learning English—prompts these recommendations. I begin with the assumption that language is not the problem. Although the chapter does not offer recipes for teaching or point to a quick fix, I hope that these recommendations will help to guide teachers in developing their own approaches to supporting mathematical reasoning and sense making for students who are learning English.

Two issues specific to English learners are crucial to consider for discussing instruction and assessment policies for this student population. First, the label "English learner" as currently used in the United States is vague, has different meanings, is not based on objective criteria, does not reflect sound classifications, and is neither comparable across states nor equivalent across settings. This label is likely to be used as a proxy for demographic labels rather than as an accurate portrayal of students who are learning English (Gándara and Contreras 2009). Second, language proficiency is a complex construct that can reflect proficiency in multiple contexts, modes, and academic disciplines. Current measures of language proficiency may not accurately reflect an individual's language competence. In particular, we do not have measures or assessments for language proficiency related to competence in mathematics for different ages or mathematical topics. These two issues—the label "English learner" and the complexities of language proficiency—can bring confusion into any discussion of mathematics instruction for students who are learning English. Thus, instructional decisions should not be made solely on the basis of the label "English learner." I will sometimes use the phrase "students who are learning English" to highlight that these students may or may not be labeled as English learners. I will also sometimes use the phrase "students who are bilingual (and may be learning English)" to emphasize that students who are learning English are also bilingual.

Generalizing about the instructional needs of all students who are learning English is difficult. Specific information about students' previous instructional experiences in mathematics is crucial for understanding how bilingual learners communicate in mathematics classrooms. Knowledge of students' experiences with mathematics instruction, language history, and educational background should guide classroom instruction. In addition to knowledge of the details of students' experiences, research suggests that high-quality instruction for English learners that supports student achievement has two general characteristics: (1) a view of language as a resource rather than a deficiency and (2) an emphasis on academic achievement, not only on learning English (Gándara and Contreras 2009).

Research provides general guidelines for instruction for this student population. Overall, English learners, students who are learning English, and bilingual students are from nondominant communities. They need access to curricula, instruction, and teachers that have proven to be effective in supporting the academic success of these students. The general characteristics of such environments are that curricula furnish "abundant and diverse opportunities for speaking, listening, reading, and writing" and that instruction "encourage students to take risks, construct meaning, and seek reinterpretations of knowledge within compatible social contexts" (Garcia and Gonzalez 1995, p. 424). Some characteristics of teachers who have succeeded with students from nondominant communities are (*a*) a high commitment to students' academic success and to student–home communication, (*b*) high expectations for all students, (*c*) the autonomy to change curriculum and instruction to meet the specific needs of students, and (*d*) a rejection of models of their students as intellectually disadvantaged. Curriculum policies for English learners in mathematics should follow the guidelines for traditionally underserved students (American Educational Research Association 2006), such as instituting systems that broaden course-taking options and avoiding systems of tracking students that limit their opportunities to learn and delay their exposure to college-preparatory mathematics coursework.

Mathematics instruction for English learners should follow the general recommendations for high-quality mathematics instruction: (*a*) students should focus on mathematical concepts and connections among those concepts, and (*b*) teachers should reinforce high cognitive demand and maintain the rigor of mathematical tasks—for example, by encouraging students to explain their problem solving and reasoning (American Educational Research Association 2006; Stein, Grover, and Henningsen 1996). Research in mathematics education ascribes two central features to teaching that promotes conceptual development: (1) teachers and students attend explicitly to concepts, and (2) students wrestle with important mathematics (Hiebert and Grouws 2007).

In particular, recommendations for supporting English learners in developing literacy (American

Educational Research Association 2004) include providing (*a*) structured academic conversation built around text and subject-matter activities to develop vocabulary and comprehension and (*b*) several years of intensive, high-quality instruction to help students master the vocabulary, comprehension, and oral language skills that will make them fully fluent in speaking, reading, and writing English.

Assessment is also important to consider for English learners, because this student population has a history of being inadequately assessed. LaCelle-Peterson and Rivera (1994, p. 56) write that English learners "historically have suffered from disproportionate assignment to lower curriculum tracks on the basis of inappropriate assessment and as a result, from over-referral to special education (Cummins 1984; Durán 1989)." Previous work in assessment has described practices that can improve the accuracy of assessment for this population. Assessment activities should match the language of assessment with the language of instruction and include measures of content knowledge assessed through the medium of the language(s) in which the material was taught (LaCelle-Peterson and Rivera 1994). Assessments should be flexible in modes (oral and written) and length of time for completing tasks.

Assessments should track content learning through oral reports and other presentations rather than relying only on written or one-time assessments. When students are first learning a second language, they can display content knowledge more easily by showing and telling rather than through reading text or choosing from verbal options on a multiple-choice test. Therefore, discussions with a student or observations of hands-on work will yield more accurate assessment data than will written assessments. Finally, evaluation should be clear on the degree to which it measures fluency of expression, as distinct from substantive content. This last recommendation raises an interesting question for assessing English learners' mathematical proficiency. For classroom assessments that are based on mathematical discussions, how can we evaluate content knowledge as distinct from fluency of expression in English? The first example in the following shows how instruction and assessment during classroom discussions can focus on mathematical content and reasoning rather than on fluency of expression in English. (Two previous publications [Moschkovich 1999, 2007a] also offer examples of focusing assessment and instruction on mathematical content and reasoning.)

Overall, research on language and mathematics education for this student population offers a few guidelines for instructional practices for teaching mathematics to English learners:

- Treat language as a resource, not a deficit (Gándara and Contreras 2009; Moschkovich 2000).
- Address much more than vocabulary and support English learners' participation in mathematical discussions as they learn English (Moschkovich 1999, 2002, 2007a, 2007b, 2007c).
- Draw on multiple resources available in classrooms—such as objects, drawings, graphs, and gestures—as well as home languages and experiences outside school.

English language learners, even as they are learning English, can participate in discussions where they grapple with important mathematical content (Moschkovich [1999] and Khisty [1995] offer example lessons). Instruction for this population should not emphasize low-level language skills over opportunities to actively communicate about mathematical ideas. One goal of mathematics instruction for students learning English should be to support all students, regardless of their proficiency in English, in participating in discussions that focus on important mathematical concepts and reasoning rather than on pronunciation, vocabulary, or low-level linguistic skills. By learning to recognize how English learners express their mathematical ideas as they are learning English, teachers can maintain a focus on mathematical reasoning as well as on language development.

Research also describes how mathematical communication is more than vocabulary. Although vocabulary is necessary, it is not sufficient. Learning to communicate mathematically is not merely or primarily a matter of learning vocabulary. During discussions in mathematics classrooms, students are also learning to describe patterns, generalize, and use representations to support their claims. The question is not whether students who are English learners should learn vocabulary but rather how instruction can best support students as they learn both vocabulary and mathematics. Vocabulary drill and practice is not the most effective instructional practice for learning either vocabulary or mathematics. Instead, experts in vocabulary and second-language acquisition find that vocabulary acquisition in a first or second language is most successful in instructional contexts that are language rich, actively involve students in using language, require both receptive and expressive understanding, and require students to use words in multiple ways over extended periods (Blachowicz and Fisher 2000; Pressley 2000). To develop written and oral communication skills, students need to participate in negotiating meaning (Savignon 1991) and in tasks that require output (Swain 2001). In sum, instruction should furnish opportunities for students to actively use mathematical language to communicate about and negotiate meaning for mathematical situations.

I will use classroom examples to address the following questions:

- How can teachers create opportunities for mathematical reasoning and sense making for high school students who are learning English?

- How can teachers use strategies that develop English learners' reasoning and sense-making skills?

- How can teachers help students communicate their reasoning effectively in multiple ways?

The following recommendations show three ways to guide mathematics instruction for English learners:

1. Focus on students' mathematical reasoning, not proficiency in English.

2. Treat home language and everyday experiences as resources, not obstacles.

3. Build on student reasoning and connect student reasoning to mathematical concepts.

First, all the examples in this chapter are of Spanish-speaking students; Latino/a mathematics learners are the focus of my research projects (this is not a coincidence, since Spanish is my own first language). All the examples come from classrooms with many Latino/a students (also not a coincidence since I conducted my research in such classrooms). Because most U.S. English learners are Latinos/as (Planty et al. 2008; Tafoya 2002), these examples are highly relevant to practices in classrooms with Latino/a English learners. However, the examples' general principles and, more important, the recommendations are not specific to Spanish or to Latino/a students. The three recommendations are relevant to *all* English learners and come from the research literature on English learners.

Second, all three examples involve students with some proficiency in English and who may be working in a bilingual mode. Thus, these are not examples of newcomers. Newcomers—students who are beginning English learners and are working in a monolingual mode in their first language—require instruction in their home language, by either a bilingual teacher or a bilingual aide. Without use of the home language, newcomers cannot benefit from mathematics instruction. The challenge of offering such bilingual instruction for newcomers is the responsibility of the school system, not of individual teachers, who for the most part are likely to be monolingual English speakers.

Finally, all the examples are of middle school or ninth-grade topics and focus on algebra readiness rather than algebra or more advanced mathematics. Again, this is a result of the focus of my research projects. Understanding students' experiences with algebra is of practical importance because algebra can be a significant barrier to educational progress, and the transition from arithmetic to algebraic thinking is a watershed where many students have trouble with or give up on mathematics. However, do not conclude from these three examples that mathematics instruction for English learners should in any way be less rigorous than that for other students or that the content for English learners should be limited to algebra readiness. In fact, schools must assess English learners in mathematics in their home language to determine the appropriate level of mathematics instruction. As mentioned, English learners have a history of inadequate assessment (LaCelle-Peterson and Rivera

1994), and these students have suffered from disproportionate assignment to lower curriculum tracks on the basis of inappropriate assessment. With proper assessment, some English learners could be placed in more advanced mathematics courses. All English learners should have access to courses that focus on rigorous mathematics content.

Focus on Students' Mathematical Reasoning, Not Proficiency in English: Describing a Pattern (Example 1)

The first example (Moschkovich 2002, 2007a) is from a classroom of grade 6–8 students in a summer mathematics class. The students constructed rectangles with the same area but different perimeters and looked for a pattern to relate the dimensions and the perimeters of their rectangles. Here is a problem similar to the one students were working on:

1. Look for all the rectangles with area 36 (length and width are integers), and write down the dimensions.
2. Calculate the perimeter for each rectangle.
3. Describe a pattern relating the perimeter and the dimensions.

This classroom had one bilingual teacher and one monolingual teacher. Four students were videotaped as they talked with each other and with the bilingual teacher (primarily in Spanish). They attempted to describe the pattern in their group and searched for the Spanish word for "rectangle." The students produced several suggestions, including ángulo [*angle*], triángulo [*triangle*], rángulos, and rangulos. Although these students attempted to find a term to refer to the rectangles, neither the teacher nor the other students supplied the correct Spanish word, rectángulo [*rectangle*].

After the small-group discussion, a second teacher (monolingual English speaker) asked several questions from the front of the class. In response, a student in this small group, Alicia, described a relationship between the length of the sides of a rectangle and its perimeter. (Transcript annotations are in brackets. Translations are in italics).

Teacher B: [Speaking from the front of the class] Somebody describe what they saw as a comparison between what the picture looked like and what the perimeter was.

Alicia: The longer the ah . . . the longer [traces the shape of a long rectangle with her hands several times] the ah . . . the longer the rángulo [rangle], you know, the more the perimeter, the higher the perimeter is.

Focusing only on this student's failed attempt to use the right word in English, "rectangle," would cause an observer to miss this student's mathematical reasoning. If we were to focus only on Alicia's inaccurate use of the term "rángulo" (although the word does not exist in Spanish, it might be best translated as "rangle," perhaps a shortening of the word "rectángulo"), we would miss how she used resources from the situation and how her statement reflects mathematical reasoning and sense making. Alicia's mathematical reasoning and sense making become visible only if we include gestures and objects as resources. This move is important for instruction because it shifts the focus from a perceived deficiency in the student that needs to be corrected—not using the word "rectangle"—to a competency that can be refined through instruction: using gestures and objects to reason mathematically. This move also shifts our attention from using the correct word in English to mathematical reasoning, as expressed not only through words but also using other modes. This shift is particularly important to uncover the mathematical reasoning in contributions from students who are learning English.

Alicia used gestures to illustrate what she meant, and she referred to the concrete objects in front of her, the drawings of rectangles, to clarify her description. Alicia also used her first language as a resource. She interjected an invented Spanish word into her statement. In this way, a gesture, objects in the situation, and the student's first language served as resources for describing a pattern. Even though the word that she used for "rectangle" does not exist in either Spanish or English, Alicia was referring to a rectangle. Her gestures showed that, even though she did not use the words "length" or "width," she was referring to the length of the side of a rectangle parallel to the floor.

Alicia's description reflects correct mathematical reasoning. The rectangle with area 36 that has the greatest perimeter (74) is the rectangle with the longest possible length, 36, and shortest possible width, 1. As the length gets longer—say, when one compares a rectangle of length 12, width 3, and perimeter 30 with a rectangle of perimeter 74—the perimeter does in fact become greater. This example illustrates how important it is to focus on a student's mathematical reasoning and not only on his or her proficiency in English. It also illustrates how gestures and objects offer resources for mathematical reasoning and sense making.

Certainly, Alicia needs to learn the word for "rectangle" (ideally in both English and Spanish), but instruction should not stop there. Rather than only correcting her use of "rángulo" or recommending that she learn vocabulary, instruction should also build on Alicia's use of gestures, objects, and description of a pattern. If instruction focuses only on what mathematical vocabulary English learners know or don't know, they will always seem deficient, because they are, in fact, learning a second language. If teachers perceive these students as deficient and only correct their vocabulary use, little room remains for addressing their mathematical reasoning, building on this reasoning, and connecting their reasoning to the discipline. English learners thus risk getting caught in a cycle of remedial instruction that does not focus on mathematical reasoning.

Treat Home Language and Everyday Experiences as Resources, Not Obstacles: Clarifying a Description (Example 2)

Whereas the first example fits the expectation that English learners struggle with vocabulary, the second illustrates how both languages—the language of the home and the language of instruction—can offer resources for mathematical reasoning. In the following discussion, students used both languages to clarify the mathematical meaning of a description. The example is from an after-school interview with two ninth-grade students. The students had been in mainstream English-only mathematics classrooms for several years. One student, Marcela, had some previous mathematics instruction in Spanish. These two students were working on the problem in figure 2.1 (see p. 23). They had graphed the line $y = -0.6x$ on paper (fig. 2.2) and were discussing whether this line was steeper than the line $y = x$.

In a conversation preceding this excerpt, Giselda had first proposed that the line was steeper and then that it was less steep. Marcela had repeatedly asked Giselda whether she was sure. In the following discussion, after Marcela proposed that the line was less steep, we see how she explained her reasoning to Giselda. (Transcript annotations are in brackets. Translations are in italics after the phrases in question.)

1   *Marcela:*   No, it's less steeper . . .

2   *Giselda:*   Why?

3   *Marcela:*   See, it's closer to the *x*-axis . . . [looks at Giselda] . . . isn't it?

4   *Giselda:*   Oh, so if it's right here . . . it's steeper, right?

5   *Marcela:*   Porque fíjate, digamos que este es el suelo. [*Because look, let's say that this is the ground.*] Entonces, si se acerca más, pues es menos steep. [*Then, if it gets closer, then it's less steep.*] . . . 'cause see this one [referring to the line $y = x$] . . . is . . . está entre el medio de la *x* y de la *y* [*is between the* x *and the* y]. Right?

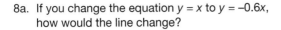

8a. If you change the equation $y = x$ to $y = -0.6x$, how would the line change?

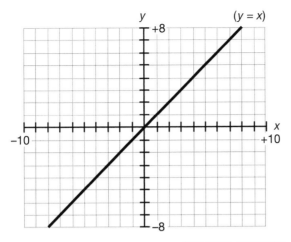

A. The steepness would change. ___ NO ___YES ___Steeper
Why or why not? ___Less steep

Fig. 2.1. Problem for example 2

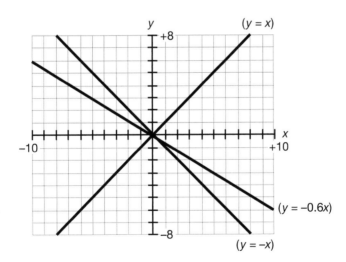

Fig. 2.2. Lines that Marcela and Giselda drew

6   *Giselda:*   [Nods in agreement.]

7   *Marcela:*   This one [referring to the line $y = -0.6x$] is closer to the x than to the y, so this one [referring to the line $y = -0.6x$] is less steep.

In this discussion, the two students were negotiating and clarifying the meanings of "steeper" and "less steep." Marcela used her first language, code switching (the practice of using two languages during one conversation or within one sentence), mathematical artifacts—the graph, the line $y = x$, and the axes—and everyday experiences as resources to reason mathematically. The premise that meanings from everyday experiences are obstacles for mathematical reasoning does not hold here. In fact, Marcela used her everyday experiences and the metaphor that the x-axis is the ground ("Porque fíjate, digamos que este es el suelo" [*Because look, let's say that this is the ground*]) as resources for making sense of this problem. Rather than finding everyday meanings as obstacles, she used an everyday situation to clarify her reasoning.

What was Marcela's mathematical reasoning? Marcela explicitly stated an assumption when she said, "Porque fíjate, digamos que este es el suelo" [*Because look, let's say that this is the ground*]. She supported her claim by making a connection to mathematical representations. She used the graph, in particular the line $y = x$ (line 5) and the axes (lines 5 and 7), as a reference to support her claim about the steepness of the line. Marcela was participating in two important aspects of mathematical reasoning: stating assumptions explicitly and connecting claims to mathematical representations.

Research does not support viewing code switching as a linguistic deficit (Valdés-Fallis 1978; Zentella 1981). In fact, the opposite is true. Although code switching has an improvised quality, it is a complex, rule-governed, and systematic language practice reflecting speakers' understanding of their community's linguistic norms. The most significant reason for a bilingual student's language choice is the language choice of the person addressing the student. We should not assume that bilingual students switch into their first language because they are missing English vocabulary or cannot recall a word. Neither should we assume that code switching is evidence of a deficiency in a student's mathematical reasoning. Code switching can offer resources for communicating mathematically (Moschkovich 2007b, 2009). For example, students sometimes code switch as they describe a mathematical situation, explain a concept, justify an answer, elaborate on an explanation, or repeat a statement.

Build on Student Reasoning and Connect Student Reasoning to Mathematical Concepts: Describing the Scales on Two Graphs (Example 3)

The third example shows how one teacher enacted instruction that promotes conceptual development by attending explicitly to concepts and allowing students to wrestle with important mathematics (Hiebert and Grouws 2007). This teacher used a mathematical discussion as an opportunity to make student reasoning visible, build on that student reasoning, and connect student reasoning to a mathematical concept. This teacher also balanced explicit attention to concepts while still allowing students themselves to wrestle with important mathematics. The teacher accomplished this not by setting a problem but by transforming student questions into a problem that makes connections.

A focus on discussions that make mathematical reasoning visible is particularly important for classrooms with students who are bilingual or learning English. On the one hand, we could imagine that mathematical discussions would be difficult to create and maintain in such classrooms. After all, if all we can see is that these students are struggling with language, we might be concerned that an emphasis on mathematical discussions will make these students look less competent than would traditional computational work. The following discussion is a counterexample to the imagined difficulties that students who are bilingual or learning English might face in discussing their mathematical reasoning. This mathematical discussion shows that bilingual students can, in fact, participate in discussions of their mathematical reasoning. The question is not whether bilingual students can engage in such discussions but how to support bilingual students in participating in discussions, making sense of mathematical concepts, and learning to communicate their reasoning. Too often, descriptions of bilingual students focus on the obstacles they face in understanding text or utterances in English, and these misunderstandings are invariably ascribed to their lack of proficiency in their second language. In contrast, the following discussion shows that we can see multiple ways of reasoning as reflecting how a student is reasoning about an important mathematical concept rather than as the result of language difficulties.

Background

Carlos and David are students in an eighth-grade bilingual class in an urban area in the United States. They are both bilingual native Spanish speakers. In this classroom, teachers and students use both languages depending on the setting and participants. The class was conducted mostly in English, with some discussions and explanations in Spanish. Carlos and David arrived in the United States from Central America as young children and have both been in a bilingual program since the early grades in elementary school. They report sometimes speaking Spanish at home, and in the classroom they seem to switch easily and fluidly between monolingual and bilingual modes (Grosjean 1999). When discussing a mathematics problem together, they sometimes used words, phrases, or extended talk in Spanish. When talking to the teacher, they used mostly English. Thus, they represent an important and significant segment of the U.S. student population: those students who would not be labeled as Spanish dominant but may still be learning academic English.

Although both students are bilingual, I selected a discussion that transpired in only one language, English, on purpose and for several reasons. First, their discussion reminds us that many conversations in bilingual classrooms take place in only one language, the language of instruction. Second, and perhaps more important, their discussion highlights how multiple ways of reasoning were not caused by using more than one language but were connected to the negotiation of mathematical meanings. I use this discussion to illustrate how the teacher built on students' mathematical reasoning and connected their reasoning to a mathematical concept. However, first I will need to show the reasoning that was taking place.

The transcript comes from a larger set of data that I collected from this classroom. (Classroom observations and videotaping were conducted during two curriculum units from *Connected Mathematics* [Lappan et al. 1998], "Variables and Patterns" and "Moving Straight Ahead." Data collected included videotapes of whole-class discussions and at least one student group for every lesson, as well as videotaped problem-solving sessions in pairs. Moschkovich [2008] analyzes this transcript in more detail, examining the multiple meanings students used for statements of the form "I went by," describing how multiple meanings and competing claims arose, showing how the students coordinated meanings with views of graph scales, and exploring the teacher's role during this discussion.)

This discussion occurred during the unit "Moving Straight Ahead" from *Connected Mathematics* (Lappan et al. 1998) toward the beginning of a classroom period. The teacher usually started the ninety-minute class with a brief whole-class discussion about a mathematics problem (the problem for that day, a problem from a previous lesson, or a homework problem). Students then worked in groups of two to four, discussing the problem at their tables. The teacher moved from group to group, asking and answering questions. Toward the end of the class period, each group usually reported or gave presentations, and the teacher led whole-class discussions. On the day of this discussion, students expected that each group would go to the front of the classroom to explain their graphs, describe how and why they solved a problem as they had, and answer questions from other students and the teacher.

The class had been working on several problems about a five-day bicycle tour. In the story, whereas some riders rode bicycles, others rode in a van and recorded the total distance from the starting point for the van every half-hour. The problem in figure 2.3 refers to the second day of the tour:

On the second day of their bicycle trip, the group left Atlantic City and rode five hours south to Cape May, New Jersey. This time, Sidney and Sarah rode in the van. From Cape May, they took a ferry across the Delaware Bay to Lewes, Delaware. Sarah recorded the following data about the distance traveled until they reached the ferry.

Time (hours)	Distance (miles)
0.0	0
0.5	8
1.0	15
1.5	19
2.0	25
2.5	27
3.0	34
3.5	40
4.0	40
4.5	40
5.0	45

1. Make a coordinate graph of the (time, distance) data given in the table.

2. Sidney wants to write a report describing day 2 of the tour. Using information from the table and the graph, what would she write about the day's travel? Be sure to consider the following questions:

   A. How far did the group travel in the day? How much time did it take them?

   B. During which interval(s) did the riders make the most progress? The least progress?

   C. Did the riders go farther in the first half or the second half of the day's ride?

3. By analyzing the table, how can you find the time intervals when the riders made the most progress? The least progress? How can you find these intervals by analyzing the graph?

Fig. 2.3. Problem: from Atlantic City to Lewes

Carlos and David often worked together in a small group. We join their discussion in progress (episodes 2–4 and with numbered lines) as they compare their answers to this problem and review the graphs that each had created independently for homework. As the discussion began, David and Carlos looked at their graphs and noticed that these graphs looked different (figs. 2.4 and 2.5).

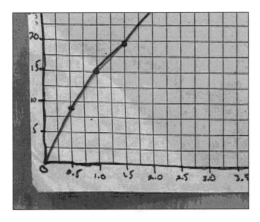

Fig. 2.4. Carlos's graph

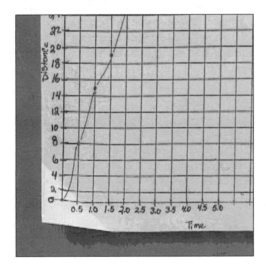

Fig. 2.5. David's graph

Carlos and David began the discussion of their solutions to the homework problem by considering whether their graphs were the same. When the teacher joined their group, Carlos asked her how they were supposed to do the graph. She responded first by asking them to compare their axes. The teacher asked the students to consider what was the same and what was different about the two graphs. She first considered whether David and Carlos had the same variable assigned to each axis and concluded that they both had put time on the *x*-axis. Next she considered what was different about the two graphs and suggested that it was how David and Carlos had "placed their numbers."

Next, the teacher and the students described the scales on their graphs. Carlos began to describe how he labeled the axes of his graph (fig. 2.4), making tick marks every two segments. In contrast, David had labeled the axes of his graph (fig. 2.5) with tick marks on every segment. (When reading the transcript, continue to refer to the graphs to understand the students' ways of making sense of the marks on the scales. Comments and gestures are in brackets.)

Episode 2: Describing the shape of the curve

42   *Carlos:*   Oh, that's true, 'cause I went by twos, I went 1, 2, . . . and then I put that one . . . he went by one.

43   [Carlos begins counting, with his right finger following the numbers on his paper.]

44   *Teacher:*   Aha, you skipped one [referring to a segment on the scale on Carlos's graph]. So how does that change how it looks?

45   *Carlos:*   Cause it doesn't go up as far, it only goes, it's more steeper. It looks more steeper.

46   [Carlos moves his right hand outward. Then he moves his right hand straight up.]

47   *Teacher:*   Remember. Similar to the difference between this one and . . . and this one here. Right?

48   [The teacher makes a sign with right thumb and index finger of her hand to show interval differences on their papers. Then she points to a graph on the blackboard. Next she points to a second graph. The first and second graphs have different scales on the *x*-axis so that the second graph is compressed along the *x* direction.]

49   *David:*   That one.

50   *Carlos:*   Yeah.

51   *Teacher:*   Here the numbers are closer together so it looks steeper. Other than that, are they the same graph?

52   [The teacher makes a sign with thumb and index finger. Then she gestures upward with her right hand.]

53   *Carlos:*   No, also here in the *x*-axis.

54   [Carlos point to the *x*-axis on his paper.]

55   [David mutters and points to the axis on his paper.]

56   *David:*   I went by twos.

57   *Carlos:*   This is the *x*-axis. Right?

58   [Carlos points to the axis.]

59   *Teacher:*   This is the *y*-axis . . . this is the *x*-axis.

60   [The teacher sweeps her pencil vertically to represent the *y*-axis and then horizontally to represent the *x*-axis.]

During episode 2, Carlos introduced the phrase "I went by twos" (line 42) to describe his own *y*-axis scale and the phrase "he went by one" (line 42) to describe David's scale. Carlos continued to use these phrases during episodes 2 and 3 as he described how he had labeled the axes of his own graph. Turning to the graphs (figs. 2.4 and 2.5), we can see that Carlos had labeled his axes by making a tick mark at every two-grid segment. In contrast, David had labeled the axes of his graph, making tick marks on every grid segment.

In episode 3, the teacher and Carlos clarified the meanings for "I went by . . . " (When reading episode 3, focus on the reasoning evident in each participant's descriptions of the scales.)

Episode 3: Using and clarifying "I went by . . . "

61	*David:*	I went by twos.
62	*Teacher:*	You went by twos and you went by [0.2 sec.].
63	*Carlos:*	I went by twos. You [didn't] . . . you went by ones! What are you talking about?
64	*Teacher:*	No, here on the *y*-axis.
65		[The teacher points to the axis.]
66	*Carlos:*	Oh, I went by fives.
67	*Teacher:*	You went by fives. . . . No, actually you didn't go by fives. You actually went by two and a halves because you'd . . . you did every 2 spaces as 5.
68		[The teacher points to Carlos's paper while she explains.]
69	*Carlos:*	Then he only went by one.
70		[Carlos points to David's paper.]
71	*Teacher:*	Every one space was two of his. You see, they're almost the same. If you look at the next two [she puts down her notebook and points to the graphs]—
72	*Carlos:*	Wait! But I don't get what you're saying.
73	*Teacher:*	OK.
74	*Carlos:*	'Cause I went by fives. [David stands up.]

During episode 3, although David and Carlos had labeled their axes differently, David initially claimed that he also "went by twos" (line 61). The teacher first accepted this claim and proceeded to describe Carlos's scale. Carlos disagreed with David, insisting that while he "went by twos," David "went by ones" (line 63). At this point Carlos seemed to notice that they might not all be talking about the same thing, saying, "What are you talking about?" (line 63). Carlos then changed the description of his own scale, saying, "Oh, I went by fives" (line 66). The teacher first agreed with this claim, saying, "You went by fives" (line 67), but then, after a short pause, she disagreed, proposing that Carlos had not gone by fives but rather had gone by "two and a halves" (line 67). In response, Carlos proposed that, if that were the case, then David "went by one" (line 69). The teacher explained that on David's scale, each space had a value of two units: "Every one space was two of his" (line 71). At this point, Carlos said that he did not understand the teacher's explanation and returned to claiming that he "went by fives" (line 74).

At the end of episode 3, the teacher focused on a detailed comparison of the two scales. By looking at the two graphs, pointing to the axes on each graph, touching the papers, and orienting the two graphs so that they were facing her, she called on the students to focus their attention on the two *y*-axis scales. During episode 4, the teacher responded to Carlos's claim that he "went by fives." In this next episode, consider these questions: How did the teacher build on students' own mathematical reasoning? How did she connect the students' mathematical reasoning to a mathematical concept?

Episode 4: Teacher responds to Carlos's claim that he "went by fives"

75	*Teacher:*	OK, your numbers, right, the numbers you have are by five . . . OK . . . If you look at one line here, what number is he at?
76		[The teacher takes David's paper and places it next to Carlos's paper and then points to David's graph.]
77	*Carlos:*	Two.
78	*Teacher:*	What number would you be at if you had a number here?
79		[The teacher points to Carlos's graph.]
80	*Carlos:*	Three.
81	*Teacher:*	Almost, two and a half.
82	*Carlos:*	Yeah.
83	*Teacher:*	Because that'd be halfway to five. OK. . . . At this point, after 1, 2, 3, he's got 6. For you after three, 1, 2, 3, you'd be at 7 and a half.
84		[The teacher counts the squares with her pencil.]
85	*Carlos:*	OK.
86	*Teacher:*	See what I mean? So it's actually two and a half. The numbers you wrote are by fives, but since you skipped a line in between, each one is two and a half.
87		[The teacher raises her hand in the air and uses her thumb and index finger to show the interval.]

These two students were making sense of the scales on their graphs in several ways. The statement "I went by twos" can be interpreted as describing the action taken to construct the scale and where the number labels were placed on the scale, so that "I went by twos" means "I went by two segments." (See fig. 2.6, Carlos's graph.)

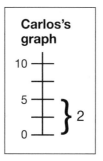

Fig. 2.6. Carlos describes his scale as "I went by twos," describing number of segments.

One could also interpret the phrase "I went by twos" as describing the quantity that the chunk created between two tick marks represented, as in "I made tick marks at every segment, and each segment represents two units." That is, the statement connects an account of constructing the graph to a quantitative relationship. For David's scale this would mean "I made tick marks at every two units." (See fig. 2.7.)

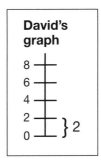

Fig. 2.7. David describes his scale as "I went by twos,"
describing number of units.

Carlos seemed to be referring to how he labeled the axes of his graph (fig. 2.4), so that tick marks appear every two segments, and to how David labeled the axes of his graph (fig. 2.5), so that tick marks appear every one segment (line 42). Carlos was thus using "went by" to refer to the value between the tick marks on the *y*-axis of his graph, five units (line 66). In contrast, the teacher was referring to the value of one segment or space in Carlos's graph, two and a halves (line 67). (See fig. 2.8)

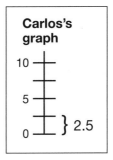

Fig. 2.8. The teacher describes Carlos's scale as going by
"two and a halves."

Table 2.1 lists three ways of using "I [or you] went by" to describe these two graphs. One meaning refers to the value of the interval between tick marks; the second, to the number of segments between tick marks; and the third, to the value of each segment between tick marks. During episodes 2 and 3, Carlos used the first and second meaning, David used the first and third meaning, and the teacher used the third meaning.

Table 2.1

Multiple meanings for "went by"

Utterance	Meaning	Students' work
Carlos: "I went by fives" David: "I went by twos"	Value of the interval between labeled tick marks	"I went by fives" Carlos's graph: 10, 5, 0 } 5 David's graph: 8, 6, 4, 2, 0 } 2 "I went by twos"
Carlos: "I went by twos" Carlos: "He [David] went by one"	Number of segments between labeled tick marks	"I went by twos" Carlos's graph: 10, 5, 0 } 2 David's graph: 8, 6, 4, 2, 0 } 1 "He went by one"
David: "I went by twos" Teacher: "You [David] went by twos . . ." Teacher: "No, actually you [Carlos] didn't go by fives, you actually went by two and a halves, because you did every two spaces as five."	Number of units in the interval between tick marks	"You went by two and a halves" Carlos's graph: 10, 5, 0 } 2.5 David's graph: 8, 6, 4, 2, 0 } 2 "I went by twos"

The teacher's role in the discussion

During this discussion, the phrase "I went by" reflected different ways of reasoning. This phrase was used with different—sometimes ambiguous, sometimes shifting—meanings that corresponded to different ways of viewing the scales. This section shows how the teacher responded to these multiple ways of reasoning and ambiguous meanings; she built on the students' reasoning and connected student reasoning to a mathematical concept: unitizing.

How did the teacher participate in this discussion? The teacher began by asking students to make sense of their graphs. She engaged the students in a discussion detailing and connecting different ways of reasoning. The teacher described how she made sense of the two graphs, sharing her reasoning as she described to the students how she saw the scale and tick marks on each graph. However, reasoning and sense making were up to not only the teacher; the students also engaged in these. The discussion revolved around what each segment or tick mark represented for each student. Thus, the teacher built her explanation on the students' own reasoning.

The teacher built on student reasoning, in part, by using the students' own language and referring to the scales as "you went by" (lines 62 and 67). She later used a different phrase, saying "you did every 2 spaces as 5" (line 67), focusing on the quantitative relationship between the spaces and the units on Carlos's graph. She also compared the two graphs, saying, "Every one space was two of his" (line 71). Last, she described the quantitative relationship between the numbers on the scale in one graph, saying, "The numbers you have are by five" (line 75). Her descriptions started out by building on students' own ways of talking and later describing students' reasoning by using a mathematical concept, unitizing.

What the teacher did and what she did not do are both important. The teacher did not produce another graph but instead based the discussion on the students' own graphs and reasoning. She did not evaluate the graphs or correct the scales. Instead, she treated both graphs as correct and accepted that multiple ways of reasoning exist. Although the teacher contested Carlos's description of his scale ("No, actually you didn't go by fives"), she also accepted his reasoning, saying, "OK, your numbers, right, the numbers you have are by five." The teacher did not explicitly define what "went by" meant or address the multiple meanings of that phrase. Instead, she made sense of what quantity each segment or tick mark represented to each student.

The teacher did not supply the correct interpretation of the scales or make an explicit contrast between the student reasoning and the right answer. Instead, she clarified and connected different ways of reasoning. She described her own reasoning to the students—how she interpreted the scales and tick marks on both graphs. For part of her descriptions, the teacher connected student reasoning to the concept of unitizing. Her descriptions focused on comparing quantities. In her descriptions, she made a distinction among labels, quantities, and measures. The teacher distinguished between the labels that go "by fives" and the value of the grid segments or spaces as a unit, saying, "You actually went by two and a halves" (line 67). In the second case, the phrase "you went by" refers to the unit value of one grid segment and is an instance of unitizing. The teacher also compared the grid segments or spaces on the two scales (line 71), again an instance of unitizing (Lamon 1994, 1996).

Finally, the teacher gave the students an opportunity to use a unitized view of the marks on the scales. She set a new problem, determining the value of the y-coordinate on each graph after moving up one grid segment on the y-axis (lines 75–82) and after moving up three grid segments on the y-axis (line 83). As she and Carlos jointly estimated the y-coordinates on the two graphs, she actively engaged him in reasoning about the scales from a unitized point of view.

Overall, the teacher used several strategies to support student reasoning: she used student-generated products; she used gestures and objects to clarify meanings; she accepted and built on students' responses; and she connected student reasoning to an important mathematical concept, unitizing. She took student reasoning seriously, ensured available time for describing and taking different points of view, and allowed room for clarification. The teacher supported this mathematical discussion by, rather than evaluating student work, describing how she understood each student's descriptions. Discussions such as the preceding, which make multiple ways of reasoning explicit and compare different meanings, can become important opportunities for students to participate in sense making and develop mathematical reasoning.

This discussion shows that multiple meanings need not be obstacles but can serve as resources for connecting to important mathematical concepts such as unitizing. This positive perspective on multiple meanings shifts the emphasis from asking what difficulties bilingual students encounter to how instruction can support bilingual students in participating in discussions. This teacher supported the mathematical discussion by using multiple interpretations, building on students' own reasoning, and connecting student reasoning to a mathematical concept. These strategies can serve as a model for engaging bilingual students in discussions that simultaneously build on student reasoning and keep the discussion connected to mathematical concepts.

This example, which transpired in only one language, English, is a model for monolingual teachers who work with bilingual students. How can this example be relevant to English learners? Most classroom discussions with English learners are likely to take place only in English because English is the language of instruction—not only because most teachers are monolingual but also because most textbooks and assessments are in English. This example also shows that teachers who work with English learners need not imagine that they must develop a new set of skills to work with English learners; they can draw on the skills they have developed for teaching native English speakers. If a teacher develops skills in supporting mathematical discussions by building on student reasoning and by connecting to concepts, he or she should also use those skills to support mathematical discussions with English learners.

References

American Educational Research Association. "English Language Learners: Boosting Academic Achievement." *Research Points* 2 (Winter 2004): 1–4.

———. "Do the Math: Cognitive Demand Makes a Difference." *Research Points* 4 (Fall 2006): 1–4.

Blachowicz, Camille, and Peter Fisher. "Vocabulary Instruction." In *Handbook of Reading Research*, edited by Michael Kamil, Peter Mosenthal, P. David Pearson, and Rebecca Barr, vol. 3, pp. 503–23. Mahwah, N.J.: Lawrence Erlbaum Associates, 2000.

Cummins, James. *Bilingualism and Special Education: Issues in Assessment and Pedagogy*. Austin, Tex.: Pro-Ed, 1984.

Durán, Richard P. "Testing of Linguistic Minorities." In *Educational Measurement*, 3rd ed., edited by Robert L. Linn, pp. 573–87. Phoenix: Oryx Press, 1993.

Gándara, Patricia, and Frances Contreras. *The Latino Education Crisis: The Consequences of Failed Social Policies.* Cambridge, Mass.: Harvard University Press, 2009.

Garcia, Eugene E., and René Gonzalez. "Issues in Systemic Reform for Culturally and Linguistically Diverse Students." *Teachers College Record* 96 (Spring 1995): 418–31.

Grosjean, François. "Individual Bilingualism." In *Concise Encyclopedia of Educational Linguistics*, edited by Bernard Spolsky, pp. 284–90. London: Elsevier, 1999.

Hiebert, James, and Doug Grouws. "The Effects of Classroom Mathematics Teaching on Students' Learning." In *Second Handbook of Research on Mathematics Teaching and Learning*, edited by Frank K. Lester Jr., pp. 371–404. Reston, Va.: National Council of Teachers of Mathematics, 2007.

Khisty, Lena Licón. "Making Inequality: Issues of Language and Meanings in Mathematics Teaching with Hispanic Students." In *New Directions for Equity in Mathematics Education*, edited by Walter Secada, Elizabeth Fennema, and Lisa Byrd Adajian, pp. 279–97. New York: Cambridge University Press, 1995.

LaCelle-Peterson, Mark, and Charlene Rivera. "Is It Real for All Kids? A Framework for Equitable Assessment Policies for English Language Learners." *Harvard Educational Review* 64 (Spring 1994): 55–75.

Lamon, Susan J. "Ratio and Proportion: Cognitive Foundations in Unitizing and Norming." In *The Development of Multiplicative Reasoning in the Learning of Mathematics*, edited by Gershon Harel and Jere Confrey, pp. 89–120. New York: SUNY Press, 1994.

———. "The Development of Unitizing: Its Role in Children's Partitioning Strategies." *Journal for Research in Mathematics Education* 27 (March 1996): 170–93.

Lappan, Glenda, James T. Fey, William M. Fitzgerald, Susan N. Friel, and Elizabeth D. Phillips. *Connected Mathematics.* White Plains, N.Y.: Dale Seymour Publications, 1998.

Moschkovich, Judit N. "Supporting the Participation of English Language Learners in Mathematical Discussions." *For the Learning of Mathematics* 19 (March 1999): 11–19.

———. "Learning Mathematics in Two Languages: Moving from Obstacles to Resources." In *Changing the Faces of Mathematics: Perspectives on Multiculturalism and Gender Equity*, edited by Walter Secada, vol. 1, pp. 85–93. Reston, Va.: National Council of Teachers of Mathematics, 2000.

———. "A Situated and Sociocultural Perspective on Bilingual Mathematics Learners." *Mathematical Thinking and Learning* 4, no. 2–3 (2002): 189–212.

———. "Beyond Words to Mathematical Content: Assessing English Learners in the Mathematics Classroom." In *Assessing Mathematical Proficiency*, edited by Alan Schoenfeld, pp. 345–52. New York: Cambridge University Press, 2007a.

———. "Bilingual Mathematics Learners: How Views of Language, Bilingual Learners, and Mathematical Communication Impact Instruction." In *Diversity, Equity, and Access to Mathematical Ideas*, edited by Na'ilah Suad Nasir and Paul Cobb, pp. 89–104. New York: Teachers College Press, 2007b.

———. "Using Two Languages when Learning Mathematics." *Educational Studies in Mathematics* 64 (February 2007c): 121–44.

———. "'I Went by Twos, He Went by One': Multiple Interpretations of Inscriptions as Resources for Mathematical Discussions." *Journal of the Learning Sciences* 17 (October 2008): 551–87.

———. "Using Two Languages when Learning Mathematics: How Can Research Help Us Understand Mathematics Learners Who Use Two Languages?" 2009. www.nctm.org/uploadedFiles/Research_News_and_Advocacy/Research/Clips_and_Briefs/Research_brief_12_Using_2.pdf (accessed November 22, 2009).

Planty, Mike, William Hussar, Thomas Snyder, Stephen Provasnik, Grace Kena, Rachel Dinkes, Angelina Kewal Ramani, and Jana Kemp. *The Condition of Education 2008* (NCES 2008-031). Washington, D.C.: National Center for Education Statistics, Institute of Education Sciences, U.S. Department of Education, 2008.

Pressley, Michael. "What Should Comprehension Instruction Be the Instruction Of?" In *Handbook of Reading Research*, edited by Michael L. Kamil, Peter B. Mosenthal, P. David Pearson, and Rebecca Barr, vol. 3, pp. 545–61. Mahwah, N.J.: Lawrence Erlbaum Associates, 2000.

Savignon, Sandra J. "Communicative Language Teaching: State of the Art." *TESOL Quarterly* 25 (Summer 1991): 261–77.

Stein, Mary Kay, Barbara W. Grover, and Marjorie Henningsen. "Building Student Capacity for Mathematical Thinking and Reasoning: An Analysis of Mathematical Tasks Used in Reform Classrooms." *American Educational Research Journal* 33 (Summer 1996): 455–88.

Swain, Merrill. "Integrating Language and Content Teaching through Collaborative Tasks." *Canadian Modern Language Review* 58 (September 2001): 44–63.

Tafoya, Sonya M. "The Linguistic Landscape of California Schools." *California Counts* 3 (February 2002): 1–15.

Valdés-Fallis, Guadalupe. "Code Switching and the Classroom Teacher." *Language in Education: Theory and Practice*, vol. 4. Wellington, Va.: Center for Applied Linguistics, 1978.

Zentella, Ana Celia. "Tá Bien, You Could Answer Me en Cualquier Idioma: Puerto Rican Code Switching in Bilingual Classrooms." In *Latino Language and Communicative Behavior*, edited by Richard Durán, pp. 109–131. Norwood, N.J.: Ablex, 1981.

Chapter 3

Minimizing Weaknesses and Maximizing Strengths of Students with Disabilities

Lisa A. Dieker, Paula Maccini, Tricia K. Strickland, and Jessica H. Hunt

Just as mathematicians are experts in various aspects of mathematics, special educators, too, have specialty areas. These areas span all grade levels and cover mild disabilities, moderate disabilities, severe profound disabilities, visual impairments, hearing impairments, physical disabilities, and behavioral challenges. Our challenge here is to address the needs of all students with disabilities in mathematics. One chapter cannot cover all aspects of mathematics for all possible types of disabilities. However, we ground our approach in the range of disabilities and the limitations of a narrow research base at the intersection of special education and mathematics to give you a strong overview. We hope our work will help you make sense of and reason about why and how students with disabilities need to be a part of secondary reform efforts. We try in this chapter to (1) discuss, in the context of the literature, the potential of having students with disabilities and special education professionals present in classrooms that are focused on reasoning and sense making and (2) offer some practical foundational examples of how to address the range of disabilities that a high school teacher might encounter in today's classroom relative to the research base. Students with disabilities must have the same opportunity and access, with the supports needed to minimize their disability and maximize their strengths in today's secondary mathematics classrooms. Although we can propose themes to consider throughout high school classrooms to ensure that students with disabilities succeed, we cannot possibly supply every idea related to every type of disability in every aspect of high school mathematics. With this more holistic approach, we begin with a foundational piece on why students with disabilities must receive instruction by content experts to truly develop reasoning and sense making in secondary mathematics.

Why Students with Disabilities Need to and Should Have Access to Advanced Mathematics Classes

At the core of this book on reasoning and sense making is the goal to help all students reach their highest potential in mathematics. For students with a range of learning, behavioral, mental, or physical disabilities, access to science, technology, engineering, and mathematics (STEM)–related careers has historically been an ongoing focus of organizations such as the Office of Special Education Programs, the Institute for Education Science, and the National Science Foundation. However, for students to have opportunities in STEM-related fields, they must first have access to high-level mathematics coursework and an opportunity to work with mathematics teachers who are both content competent and pedagogically proficient. The road for students with disabilities to have access to such teachers and mathematics opportunities has been uphill. In recent years, as schools have been held accountable for this subpopulation of students making achievement gains in mathematics (i.e., adequate yearly progress), access has become less of an issue, as has been finding ways for successful instruction of this population.

Although we have framed the chapter in the context of giving students equitable opportunities in mathematics, we would be remiss if we did not mention that before students can enter STEM fields, they must first have access to science and mathematics. We also see that every day, new technological advances emerge that could help level the opportunities for students with disabilities to have access to mathematics. Until students have access to advanced courses and are given tools to maximize their strengths and minimize their weaknesses in mathematical reasoning and sense making, the E and T in STEM are not even available to most students with disabilities: both engineering and technology require access to advanced mathematics. Keeping in mind the current status of the field for students with disabilities in STEM areas, we give a brief history of the progression of opportunities for students with disabilities in mathematics. Then we examine the trend to educate and evaluate students with disabilities in the same way as their nondisabled peers in mathematics, how lack of access to mathematics has affected learning gains, how the focal points offer a role for depth to prepare students for reasoning and sense making, and what the research tells us about teaching students with disabilities in mathematics.

How Special Education Evolved in Gaining Access to Mathematics

With respect to litigation and legislation, the historical evolution of the rights of persons with disabilities in educational settings has occurred systematically, with each step moving closer to equality in both opportunities and education. In the past fifty-plus years, since the equality decision of *Brown v. Board of Education* (1954), schools and society have become progressively more inclusive. In 1965 the Elementary and Secondary Education Act (ESEA) set forth funding for children with disabilities and children who were economically disadvantaged to participate in state-initiated educational programs (Heward 2003). Before 1975, students with disabilities did not have the right to even attend school, let alone equal opportunity for access to mathematics classes. However, in 1975 Congress passed the Education for All Handicapped Children Act, guaranteeing the inclusion of persons with disabilities in federally funded programs (which included schools) and giving them a free and appropriate public education within the least restrictive environment (Heward 2003).

Further litigation and corresponding laws have continued advancing ideas of access, equality, and identification. In 1997, amendments to the Individuals with Disabilities in Education Act (IDEA) ensured access to the general education curriculum (1997), while the reauthorization of the act in 2004 aligned exceptional education policy with mainstream educational policy to ensure equitable educational experiences for all students (IDEIA [U.S. Department of Education 2004]).

Through five decades of changing laws and litigation, legislative action afforded persons with disabilities not only funding but also equal access to education in the general classroom. Further litigation brought to bear the issue of proper identification, classification, and defining characteristics for persons with disabilities to receive appropriate educational services. Ideas of an appropriate education as well as models of identification underwent major changes. Persons with disabilities received increased services in inclusive general education classrooms and at the same time were held accountable to a master standards-based curriculum moving toward full equality in educational access and outcomes.

Less Opportunity to Learn Leads to Poorer Achievement

One can partially credit disparities for students with disabilities to their diminished opportunity to learn mathematics and their not having the same access to teachers or standards (fig. 3.1). Consider a student who has not mastered his or her basic multiplication and related division facts. Before the emphasis on high-stakes testing, while other students were being exposed to concepts such as balancing equations or geometry standards, a special educator pulled out many students with disabilities and asked them to continue to work on mastering these basic facts. Students do need fluency in their foundational computation skills. But the belief that students must establish fluency in skills (a weakness for some students) before having any opportunity to learn advanced skills is one reason the disparities in access to advanced mathematics courses exist for students with disabilities. Special education teachers are certified and extremely competent in their profession but, just like mathematics teachers, are not equal in all areas of mathematics: separately, neither mathematics nor special education teachers have all the knowledge they need to prepare students with disabilities well. Special educators often have limited backgrounds in mathematics, whereas mathematics educators often have less knowledge related to working with students with disabilities (Dieker and Berg 2002).

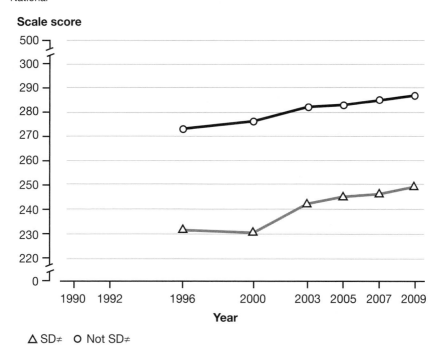

Average scale scores for mathematics, grade 8, by disability status of student, including 504 [IEP] for jurisdiction: 1990, 1992, 1996, 2000, 2003, 2005, 2007, and 2009

National

Fig. 3.1. Scores of grade 8 students with (open triangles) and without (open circles) disabilities in mathematics

If these limitations contribute to a lack of opportunity and a lack of highly qualified instruction, what is the solution? We recognize that the following suggestion is not easy to implement; however, students with disabilities should have the opportunity to work with highly qualified mathematics teachers as much as possible. Also, remedial skills should be compensated for as much as possible through using calculators, manipulatives, multiplication tables, formula charts, and any other tool that helps students attend to the curriculum and keep up with their nondisabled peers (or minimize their disabilities) in the standard mathematics curriculum. The expectation would be that students with disabilities would have highly qualified professionals who would ensure that their needs are accommodated and yet teach them according to the same high standards for their nondisabled peers.

Access and Assessment for Students with Disabilities

The issues for students with disabilities parallel those of students without disabilities who move around from school to school or who lack access to strong teachers. For example, a nondisabled student moving from state to state may experience inconsistencies in how he or she is taught mathematics in the elementary grades. This issue is then compounded for students with disabilities. If in one setting a certified mathematics teacher instructs a student and in another this student learns in a self-contained classroom from a teacher who may not possess the necessary content knowledge, the student may not develop understanding of the same core knowledge. Thus, for students with disabilities, both a lack of consistency in what is taught and the teacher's environment and content area expertise compound the mobility issue.

Students' taking state assessments that often determine placement presents a third and further compounding issue. With the current Common Core State Standards initiative, hope exists that what will be taught to students with disabilities will be the same in all settings. However, to address this common core at the secondary level for students with disabilities, special education professionals must receive side-by-side training and further content knowledge development to ensure that students with disabilities can master these standards. Also, special education can no longer offer segregated instruction that is not grounded in the core curriculum, or else students with disabilities will not be able to access the high school mathematics curriculum. Along with similar instruction and consistency in the content that students with disabilities receive, a need also exists for consensus in how students with disabilities will be assessed on the common core at both state and national levels. In some states, students can use assistive devices on parts of mathematics tests (e.g., calculators). In other states, students can use tools such as a list of formulas and extended time; still other states allow nothing. Inconsistencies in service can lead to a lack of clarity about student performance because of the different ways that students must demonstrate their knowledge. Special education is founded on individualization (hence the use of an individualized education program), yet states, districts, and schools negate this individualized process in the name of budgets, for teacher convenience, or for a common assessment that ignores individualized needs. All students have individualized needs, but students without disabilities have found ways to compensate for differences, usually without supports, which may not be possible for a student with a disability.

Trend to Educate and Evaluate Students with Disabilities

Recent and current legislative mandates such as the pending reauthorization of ESEA (2010) and IDEIA (2004) all espouse higher academic standards for all students and holding public schools accountable for student proficiency toward meeting those standards. All students must have access to the same curriculum as their nondisabled peers and be taught by highly qualified teachers. Mathematics education offerings should also include empirically validated methods to help improve student performance and help to increase the achievement of students with and without disabilities. For accountability, Title I of the ESEA requires each state to assess students in three content areas (i.e., mathematics, reading or language arts, and science) annually in grades 3–8 and at least once more between grades 10 and 12. Title I specifies certain requirements for these assessments. First, the same academic assessments are administered to all students, including students with disabilities. These assessments must also align with the state's academic content and student academic achievement standards and must assess higher-order thinking skills and understanding. All students must participate in these assessments; however, students with disabilities must have access to reasonable adaptations and accommodations. Typical accommodations include alternative presentation (e.g., enlarged print or Braille), options for response mode (e.g., writing answers in the test book rather than on the answer sheet or letting them dictate responses), extended time, and alternative settings (e.g., taking the test in a separate room). Results from these assessments must be reported with disaggregation of scores for students with disabilities. In an effort to increase the achievement of students with disabilities, Title I specifically holds states accountable for these students' continuous and substantial improvement.

In 2004, Congress reauthorized IDEA and included changes that align with ESEA (which was previously known as No Child Left Behind). The 2004 IDEIA regulations require states to establish goals for students with disabilities that are consistent, to the extent appropriate, with academic standards for all children in the state, and states must report annually on progress toward meeting these goals. Students with disabilities may receive accommodations to enable them to participate in the general education curriculum and in state and district assessments. If a student cannot participate in a state or district assessment, even with appropriate accommodations, an alternative assessment must be developed (McLaughlin and Thurlow 2003).

NCTM Focal Points and High School Focus Document Provide for Greater Secondary Access

If adopted consistently for teacher preparation in both special education and secondary education, the National Council of Teachers of Mathematics (NCTM) Curriculum Focal Points should help increase the achievement of students with disabilities and give them more access to higher-level mathematics with a focus on reasoning and sense making. Why do we see the Focal Points as a tool to help promote advanced mathematics? Because instead of allowing students to be stuck on a skill such as multiplication facts for life, we should compensate for any lack of understanding by allowing them to access additional concepts—the focal points at the next grade level. NCTM's *Curriculum Focal Points for Prekindergarten through Grade 8 Mathematics: A Quest for Coherence* (2006) focuses on areas of emphasis and describes the most significant mathematical concepts and skills at each grade level. Since the grade-level focal points focus on important mathematical concepts and create a structure for curriculum design, instruction, and assessment at each grade level, adaptations and modifications can be developed at any point related to a roadblock to learning. The Focal Points did not intend to offer specific instructional methods, materials, or recommendations for professional development; therefore, special education needs ongoing research to promote the progress of students with disabilities through these essential skills.

Demonstrating mastery of the Focal Points before entering high school or having access to tools to compensate for missing skills is crucial for students with disabilities. More than half (56 percent) of the students with emotional or behavioral disorders are at least three levels behind students without disabilities in mathematics (Bottge, Rueda, and Skivington 2006). Similarly, students with learning disabilities (LD) are two grade levels behind students without disabilities in mathematics, leveling off around the fifth-grade achievement level (Butler et al. 2003).

NCTM's 2008 Position Statement on Equity in Mathematics Education focuses on ensuring that all students have equitable access to "challenging, rigorous, and meaningful mathematical experiences," which may be different from recognizing and accepting all the factors that influence a disability (e.g., language, memory, behavior) and consequently the academic achievement of students.

Characteristics inherent to students with disabilities can hinder their learning of mathematical concepts. Allsopp and colleagues (2003) highlighted four characteristics that may affect the development of mathematical understanding: (1) attention problems, (2) cognitive-processing problems, (3) memory problems, and (4) metacognitive deficits. Also, the nature of how students with disabilities are educated may have implications for their effectiveness in secondary mathematics. The most recent data posted on the Data Accountability Center Web site (2007) showed that approximately 24 percent of students with behavioral challenges spent less than 40 percent of the school day in the general education classroom, whereas 30 percent of students with learning disabilities spent between 40 and 79 percent of their classroom time in general education settings. Wehby, Lane, and Falk (2003) point out that not only do students with behavior disorders in self-contained classrooms receive academic instruction for only 30 percent of the school day, but the teachers responsible for the academic instruction also typically do not have in-depth content area knowledge.

The intention of the Curriculum Focal Points is to ensure equal access to a high-quality mathematics education for all students by targeting three mathematical concepts in a logical, systematic order in each grade level. However, a lack of access to high-quality mathematics instruction rooted in the Focal Points may marginalize access to higher-level mathematics. Students with disabilities need access to an advanced mathematics curriculum taught by content teachers with in-depth knowledge at the high school level while also receiving academic or behavioral supports and services to minimize their weaknesses and to maximize their strengths.

To introduce the concept of minimizing weaknesses, we use information from "Developing Reasoning Habits in the Classroom" in *Focus in High School Mathematics* (NCTM 2009, p. 11), which is recommended as the foundation of a classroom that supports reasoning and sense making. We have also proposed adaptations to and accommodations for these particular strategies that might be necessary for various types of disabilities.

Table 3.1 offers suggestions to high school teachers to adapt for students' disabilities in the classroom. The leftmost column lists the NCTM language related to creating a classroom that promotes reasoning habits. The columns after each suggestion propose ideas for how to accommodate a student with any of the following needs: visual, auditory, physical, verbal, behavioral, or memory/processing issues. This list is not comprehensive but rather suggests initial ideas to ensure that your classroom is accepting of all types of learners. The suggestions encompass students who have disabilities that might affect their involvement in rich reasoning and sense-making environments.

To implement any lesson we recommend, teachers assume that they will be instructing a student who cannot walk, talk, see, hear, or behave—really employing principles of Universal Design for Learning (UDL), a concept that embraces inclusive settings (see www.cast.org for UDL resources). When instruction is created initially in a way that meets the needs of students with disabilities (from our experience and observation of thousands of mathematics classrooms), the learning for all students—not just students with disabilities—increases. With these thoughts in mind, consider how your efforts to create a classroom that is rich in reasoning and sense making embrace the needs of the range of students with disabilities in general education mathematics classrooms.

Existing Research for Teaching High School Students with Mathematics Disabilities in Relation to Reasoning and Sense Making

Recent reviews of the literature (Maccini, Mulcahy, and Wilson 2007; Maccini et al. 2008; Strickland and Maccini 2010) have shown that several strategies help to improve mathematics performance for secondary students with disabilities. Table 3.1 presents these strategies in relation to six areas of

Table 3.1

Adaptations to develop reasoning habits in the classroom

NCTM recommendation	Adaptations (by type of disability or deficit)					
	Visual	Auditory	Physical	Verbal	Behavioral	Memory/processing
Provide tasks that require students to figure things out for themselves.	Ensure that tasks have written and auditory components.	Ensure that visual images are part of the task.	Ensure that materials used (e.g., larger blocks) and space for work are accessible and easy to handle.	Repeat procedures; ask students in the groups to check understanding of peers.	Establish a positive peer group to discuss task. Foster positive reinforcement for on-task behavior.	Give concrete examples of steps within the task to help the student put it all together.
Ask students to restate the problem in their own words, including any assumptions they have made.	No adaptations needed.	Have students write their statements as well as give them orally.	Ensure that the student can see/hear as others share their thoughts.	Use assistive technology to share student's thoughts in text-to-speech format.	Ensure that student has processing time and will be able to share thoughts in a positive climate.	Allow student to write down response before sharing.
Give students time to analyze a problem intuitively, explore the problem further by using models, and then proceed to a more formal approach.	Remember that a student processing through only one modality may need more time; ensure that models are presented physically or orally—if possible, furnish 3D models for tactile input.	Remember that a student processing through only one modality may need more time; ensure that models are presented physically or orally and with written phrases.	Ensure that all workspace is accessible and that students can access models.	No adaptations needed.	Use a timer so that students have a concept of how much time they have to complete the task; list the steps of what they are to do within each allotted block of time.	Clarify any language that may delay processing and ensure that the student can make a basic statement about the problem before moving forward.
Resist the urge to tell students how to solve a problem when they become frustrated; find other ways to support.	Ensure that you present verbal information for understanding.	Ensure that you present enough visual information for understanding.	Ensure that physical limitations do not impair ability to understand.	Ensure that this student has a way to share his or her thoughts through pictures (e.g., Google images) or through text-to-speech technology.	Monitor frustration levels to ensure success and avoid a behavioral outburst. Furnish scaffolding to ensure moving forward and to avoid frustration.	Check that the language or the processing speed of dialogue is not impairing students' ability to understand.
Ask students questions that will prompt their thinking—for example, "Why does this work?" or "How do you know?"	Stand near or give student a cue for a question addressed to him or her.	Offer both oral and written summaries of questions (e.g., overhead, whiteboard); use another student to make visual images of questions on the board.	Allow ways to respond besides raising hand (e.g., have student with physical disability move forward).	Allow students other ways to answer questions (e.g., whiteboard, text-to-speech format, images).	To decrease anxiety, prepare student for direct questions; ensure that the student gets positive reinforcement from you and peers throughout questioning.	Use cues such as standing near a student before asking a question or supply two questions the student can answer ahead of time.

Table 3.1—*Continued*
Adaptations to develop reasoning habits in the classroom

NCTM recommendation	Adaptations (by type of disability or deficit)					
	Visual	Auditory	Physical	Verbal	Behavioral	Memory/processing
Allow adequate wait time after a question for students to formulate their own reasoning.	Ensure that student is seated where he or she can hear the question clearly; repeat student questions for the class.	Ensure time for student to process the written question or allow time for the sign language interpreter.	No adaptations needed.	Ensure that student has a way to share thoughts or to clarify if he or she does not understand.	Ensure that student is attending to you as you pose the question; ask student to repeat the question if you feel that he or she was not focused.	Use wait-time research; if student has a language-processing issue, consider doubling wait time.
Encourage students to ask probing questions to themselves and one another.	Ensure adequate physical representation of concept if questions are related to a visual image.	Allow students to use assistive devices or interpreter for sharing questions.	No adaptations needed.	Allow student to use assistive devices or interpreter for sharing questions.	Offer examples of appropriate questions and ensure positive peer interactions.	Help students word questions or to process information as needed.
Expect students to communicate their reasoning to their classmates and the teacher orally and in writing by using proper mathematical vocabulary.	Establish rules for turn taking for a student who cannot see hands raised, body language, and the like. Ensure that written questions are in an accessible format.	Educate class on students' use of an interpreter or lip reading to ensure equal participation.	Supply accessible table and materials in the group setting; ensure use of appropriate assistive devices for written work.	Furnish a way for students who have limited speech to share questions (e.g., voice to text) and educate peers on how to work effectively with such students.	Offer a safe way for student to participate and minimize any possibility of negative peer feedback or potential anger through the reasoning process.	Ensure that the student understands key vocabulary words to participate in a group setting; assist with scribing responses if processing language is difficult.
Highlight exemplary explanations and have students reflect on what makes them effective.	Ensure that all students are celebrated for how they learn and contribute to the classroom.					
Establish a classroom climate in which students feel comfortable sharing their mathematical arguments and productively critiquing the arguments of others.	Establish rules for sharing that include oral cues.	Establish rules for sharing that include visual cues.	Ensure that the climate allows those with physical limitations to participate.	Ensure that students can be engaged in ways beyond oral responses (e.g., by writing on dry-erase boards).	Discuss and role-play how to give and receive feedback to arguments. Have daily social goals grounded in this area for all students.	Ensure that the climate allows time to process questions, contribute to group discussions, and write responses.

difficulty, including the following: (*a*) concrete–semiconcrete–abstract graduated instructional sequence (Maccini and Hughes 2000; Maccini and Ruhl 2000; Scheuermann, Deshler, and Schumaker 2009; Witzel, Mercer, and Miller 2003); (*b*) strategy instruction to assist with self-monitoring academic performance (Maccini and Hughes 2000; Maccini and Ruhl 2000); (*c*) problems anchored in real-world applications (Bottge, Heinrichs, Chan, et al. 2001; Bottge, Rueda, LaRoque, et al. 2007; Bottge, Rueda, Serlin, et al. 2007; Maccini and Hughes 2000; Maccini and Ruhl 2000); (*d*) technology (CITEd 2007); (*e*) grouping for instruction (Allsopp 1997); and (*f*) graphic organizers (Ives 2007).

We present two modified examples that reflect aspects of the research about students with disabilities from *Focus in High School Mathematics: Reasoning and Sense Making* (NCTM 2009). Both examples highlight integrating these empirically validated practices to support and extend students' reasoning and sense making in the general education math curriculum for students with special needs. Example 1 addresses number systems and the distributive property and the bridge from the area model of multiplication with integers to polynomials. Example 2 demonstrates how one can extend the area model in the first example to geometrically represent quadratics and completing the square. Both examples include a mnemonic designed to help students organize their thought processes and the use of multiple representations (i.e., manipulatives, graphic organizer, and contextualized problems) to help students organize their thought processes while setting up and solving for the solution. However, the instructional focus is to help students make sense of mathematics and to offer many access points within the lesson for students to apply reasoning and sense making. We caution you to avoid overemphasizing mnemonics and metaphors and to give students ample opportunity to engage with the mathematics first and use these tools once reasoning and sense making about a concept have been achieved. Such tools can help students with deficits in organization and memory after they clearly understand the mathematical concepts. Both examples address the areas of difficulty that table 3.1 describes.

Example 1

Original task from *Focus in High School Mathematics* ("A Model Idea," p. 27)—Create an area model for the product of expressions: *A*(*B* + *C*).

Background: Students have previously explored the area model of multiplication with integers.

Adapted task: Jamaica is planning to expand her bedroom to include a den for her new desk and computer. Her bedroom's dimensions are 10 ft. × 12 ft. She plans to keep the width of 12 ft. for both rooms the same, and she has no restrictions on the length (*L*) of the den. Show an expression that represents the total area of the bedroom and new den. You can write symbols, draw a picture, and/or use the algebra tiles to help you.

Teacher calls on student 1 to read the problem aloud.

Teacher:	What can we do to help us understand the problem?
Student 1:	I need to read the problem again and write down what I know. I know the length of the bedroom is 10 ft. and the width is 12 ft. [*The student reads the STAR cue card {see next page} and writes down responses.*]
Teacher:	Excellent. Great work using the STAR strategy and writing down what you know and need to find! We know the dimensions of the bedroom so far. What else do we know?

STAR Strategy Cue Card	

1. Search the word problem.
    a. Read the problem carefully.
    b. What do I know? What do I need to find?
 	
2. Translate.
    a. Represent the problem (use symbols,
    pictures, algebra tiles, etc.).
 	
3. Answer.
 	
4. Review the problem.
    a. Reread the problem.
    b. Does the answer make sense? Why?
    c. Check answer.
	I know the length of the bedroom is 10 ft. × 12 ft. . . .

Student 2:   Jamaica is going to add a den to her bedroom for a study room for her computer and desk. We know the area: length times width.

Student 1:   I don't know. I don't know how much she is going to add on.

Student 2:   It's *L*. She can add on any length, right?

Teacher: Do you all agree? [*Teacher writes student 2's ideas on the board.*]

Student 1:   Oh yeah. But she has the same width for both rooms.

Teacher: Show me your ideas so far—or translate them by using symbols, using the algebra tiles, or drawing a picture.

Student 1:   I am going to use tiles. I'll put down 10 tiles for the length—the light gray tiles because they are the constants and 12 tiles for the width. I don't know how long the den is, but I can use a dark gray tile for her den. I can use an *X*-Bar for the length (*L*) for Jamaica's den. I know that 10 tiles times 12 tiles is 120 light gray tiles, and I will have 12 dark gray tiles because 1 constant times *L* equals *L*.

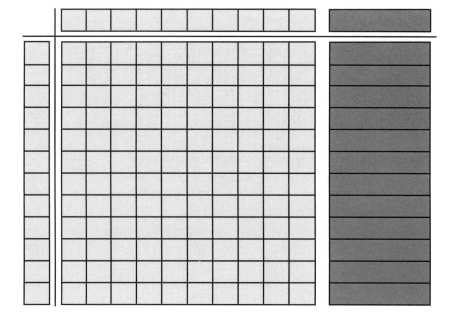

Student 2:   I filled in the boxes to show the area. I multiplied 12 ft. by 10 ft. and know the area of the bedroom is 120 square feet. I let *L* represent length of the new den and know that it is the same width as the bedroom and wrote it in the second box.

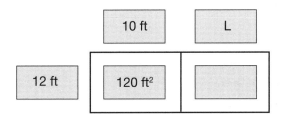

Student 2:   So my answer is 12 ft. (10 ft. × *L*).

Student 1:   I think it's 120 light gray squares and 12 dark gray tiles for the answer. [*Student writes down answer on the STAR worksheet under "Answer."*]

Teacher: Are these the same? Why or why not? [*The teacher cues students to the last step in the STAR strategy: "Review the problem."*]

Student 1:   I counted the light gray area, and it is 120 square tiles. It's correct because I have 10 times 12, which is 120. I have 12 dark gray tiles because 1 blue tile times 12 is 12 dark gray tiles. My answer shows that Jamaica will have 120 ft.^{2} + 12*L*.

Student 2:   I got 12 ft.^{2} (10 ft. + *L*) because I found the area of the product of the width of 12 ft. times the length of 10 ft. + *L*. Then I multiplied. See inside my boxes! I got 120 ft.^{2} + 12*L*. This is similar to what we did with multiplying integers, but we have *L* to represent the length of the new den, that's all.

Teacher: Great work. You showed the distributive property [*teacher writes "distributive property" on the board*] and area as a product and the area as the sum with polynomials. [*The teacher continues to explore the area model for other products, such as (x + 2)(x + y + 5), and encourages students to create different models with graph paper or organizers or tiles to make connections; the teacher checks with two students to assess their frustration level and overall understanding.*]

Example 2

Original task from *Focus in High School Mathematics* ("Squaring It Away," p. 36)—Find a way of solving the equation $x^2 + 10x = 144$ by using an area model.

Adapted task: The area of Dan's bedroom is 144 square feet. The length is 10 feet longer than the width. What are the measurements of Dan's bedroom?

Teacher: Let's use our STAR strategy to explore this problem. Everyone take out your cue card. To *search* the problem, let's read this problem together.

Students: [*Choral reading of problem {one student uses a computer to participate in reading the problem}.*]

Teacher: With your partner(s), discuss what you know about the problem and what we need to find out.

Students discuss the problem with their partner(s) as the teacher walks around the room, asking prompting questions and monitoring frustration levels as needed.

Teacher:	So, who can tell me what we know?
Student 1:	The area equals 144 square feet.
Student 2:	We need to multiply the length times the width to get the area.
Teacher:	Great! Now, what do we need to find out?
Student 1:	What are the measurements of Dan's bedroom?
Teacher:	What exactly does that mean?
Student 2:	How many feet equal the length and the width of Dan's bedroom.
Teacher:	Do you agree? And remember to tell me why.
Student 1:	I guess so. Yeah, that makes sense because we multiply the length and the width to get the area. So we need to know what numbers to multiply to get 144.
Teacher:	Excellent! Now, using our STAR strategy, let's translate what we know into mathematical representations. Work with your partner(s) to determine how to do this. Remember, you can use algebra tiles, drawings, and/or symbols.

Students discuss the problem with their partner(s) as the teacher walks around the room, asking prompting questions and monitoring processing and frustration levels.

Teacher:	Okay, let's hear from some groups. How did your group translate this problem? Remember to tell us why you chose to translate the problem the way you did.
Student 1:	We used tiles. We don't know numbers for the width or the length, so we used an *X-Bar* to represent the width and an *X-Bar* plus 10 constants to represent the length. Since it's area, we need to multiply. Can I show you what we did? I can't explain it.
Teacher:	Sure! Come up and use the overhead tiles.
Student 1:	Okay, here's what we did.

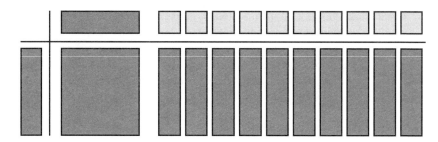

Teacher:	Class, what do you think about that? [*The teacher allows wait time before asking— standing near one student who she knows has the right answer as a cue that she will call on him.*]
Student 2:	Yeah, that works. We used a variable, x, to represent the width and the algebraic expression $x + 10$ to represent the length. It's the same thing. But we wrote an equation, $x(x + 10) = 144$.
Student 1:	We don't have 144. That's a lot of tiles, and where do we put them?
Teacher:	You may not have 144 constants, but are the 144 square units represented in this model?
Student 2:	Yes. All the tiles inside the cross bars *equal* 144. So, another way to write my equation is $x^2 + 10x = 144$.
Teacher:	Class, do you agree? Tell me how you know this [*the teacher allows wait time before calling on a student*].

Spend time exploring the issue of equality, if needed; ensure that any students with processing issues grasp the concept before moving forward.

Teacher: Okay, we have *searched* the problem and *translated* the problem; now we need to an-swer the problem. Any ideas how we can do this?

Student 1: I don't see how the tiles can help solve this problem.

Student 2: Maybe if we can find the area of a square, we can just take the square root.

Student 1: But this is a rectangle, not a square.

Teacher: Is there a way to rearrange our tiles so that we get a figure similar to a square? Work on this with your partner(s).

Students discuss the problem with their partner(s) as the teacher walks around the room, asking prompting questions as needed. Students can concretely manipulate the tiles to create a shape simi-lar to a square.

Teacher 1: Okay, what did you find?

Student 1: We can divide the 10 constants in half and rearrange the tiles like this. Then we can add constants to complete the square. [*The student shows her work as she talks.*]

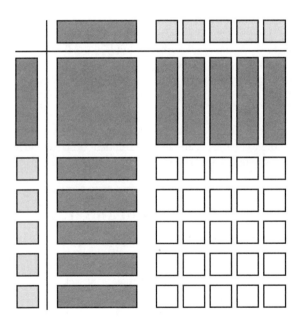

Student 2: If we added 25 to the tiles, we will need to add 25 to the equation. So, now we have $x^2 + 10x + 25 = 144 + 25$, or $x^2 + 10x + 25 = 169$.

Teacher: Can we take the square root of $x^2 + 10x + 25$?

Student 2: Is it $x + 5$?

Teacher: Why do you think that may be?

The teacher asks the students to write their process on the board as they explain; doing so affords verbal and visual options for students during the discussion.

Student 2: Well, we multiplied $x + 5$ by $x + 5$, so we squared it and got $x^2 + 10x + 25$. So the square root must be $x + 5$.

Student 1: I just found the square root of 169 by using my calculator. It's 13. So, $x + 5 = 13$, which means that $x = 8$, because $8 + 5 = 13$.

Student 2: Wait! Negative 13 squared is also 169. So, if $x + 5 = -13$, then $x = -18$. Wait—that doesn't make sense. You can't have a negative measurement.

Student 1: But we totally changed the shape of Dan's bedroom when we created a square instead of a rectangle. So, does it matter if we have a negative measurement?

Student 2: Yeah, it matters. Let's check our answer. If $x = 8$, then the width of Dan's bedroom is 8 feet and the length is 18 feet. Eight times 18 equals 144. It works! If you plug a -8 into my equation, it doesn't work. See, $64 - 80$ does not equal 144.

Teacher: Thank you for reviewing your answer! In our STAR strategy, we *review* our answer by asking whether our answer makes sense and checking it with the original problem.

Student 1: Can you just find the measurements of Dan's bedroom by guessing and checking? I can just substitute values in for x until I find one that works.

Teacher: Can you explain this further?

Student 1: Well, I first tried having a width of 10. That makes the length 20. Therefore, $10(10 + 10) = 200$, not 144, so my first guess is too high. So I tried 5 as the width. Therefore, $5(5 + 10) = 75$. This is too low, so I chose the width of 8 and the length of 18, which equals 144, so my measurements are correct. [*Again, student is writing on the board for all students to see the process.*]

Teacher: Great observations! The process of adding a constant to a quadratic expression so that it becomes a perfect square is called "completing the square." This is a strategy we can use for quadratics other than this word problem. So, it's an important strategy that we will continue to explore. The guess-and-check strategy for solving this problem is also valid. Let's continue to explore multiple ways of solving quadratics.

Throughout both examples, teacher talk is low and student engagement is high. This type of student engagement—being able to hear, see, and listen to student thinking during reasoning and sense making—is vital for students with disabilities in an inclusive classroom.

Access to a High-Stakes Curriculum and Integrating What We Know about Best Practice

Through empirically supported instructional practices and reasoning and sense making, students with disabilities gain access to the general education mathematics curriculum. For example, instruction can incorporate a general problem-solving strategy, STAR, to cue students to connect the mathematics tasks to their existing knowledge, to address sense making, and to prompt students to justify their answers. Students are also encouraged to explore the math task by using concrete manipulatives, pictorial representations, and/or abstract notation, which allows multiple entry points. Also, empirically supported instructional practices give students with disabilities scaffolds to engage in the general education curriculum. For example, concrete manipulatives, cue cards, graphic organizers, and technology support multiple entry points and compensate for deficits in computation, cognitive processes, and metacognition. Examples 1 and 2 incorporate instructional practices (i.e., the concrete–semiconcrete–abstract sequence, strategy instruction, real-world context, peer-assisted instruction, graphic organizers, and technology) that are empirically supported in the special education algebra literature for students with LD (Maccini et al. 2008; Strickland and Maccini 2010). The teacher also scaffolds by using questions and having students compare and justify their strategies for solving the problem.

In example 1, students choose different approaches to represent the problem, given their individual student characteristics. Student 1 chooses the algebra tiles to help him to visualize area. Once he represents the problem with tiles, he counts the number of light and dark gray tiles that form the area of the rectangle. Student 2 chooses a semiconcrete representation by means of a graphic display to represent the area of both the bedroom and the extension of the den. The student experiences organizational difficulties and uses the diagram to help organize the information before finding the area as both the product and the sum.

In example 2, the teacher encourages students to work with peers to engage in reasoning and sense making; however, the groupings must be carefully arranged. Although pairing a higher-ability student with a lower-ability student is recommended (Access Center 2004), teachers should control pairings for vast ability differences (Allsopp 1997). For example, student 2 excels in algebra; however, student 1 needs more support. Student 1 relies on concrete manipulatives, which are easy to manipulate; remove the burden of computation; and allow him to express his sense making in an alternative, nonverbal manner. Also, student 1 uses a guess-and-check strategy to complete the task. Student 2, however, thinks abstractly and determines the measurements of the bedroom through algebraic manipulation. However, he can link his equation to the algebra tiles. Students 1 and 2 are not initially paired because of the differences in their ability levels. However, they can engage in discourse during the group discussion as a result of teacher facilitation. By engaging in the task in various ways in a classroom, students can discuss the reasonableness of their methods as well as the solutions, and students of various ability levels can engage in discourse. Table 3.1 includes many ideas to ensure that all students succeed in a secondary mathematics classroom focused on reasoning and sense making.

What Research Tells Us about Teaching Students with Disabilities in Mathematics and How It Relates to Reasoning and Sense Making

Mathematics, especially algebra, has historically been a challenge for many students with disabilities. Maccini and Hughes (2000) discussed the challenges that students with disabilities face in mathematics, including considerable difficulty, lower enrollment in advanced mathematics classes, and a lack of opportunities beyond high school. All students can benefit from student-centered classrooms, inquiry-based learning, and peer discourse. Other tools that the mathematics education literature notes as effective practice in special education include anchored instruction (Bottge et al. 2001), hands-on learning, and group work (Maccini and Hughes 2000). If students with disabilities are served in the general education mathematics classroom, special educators must understand the areas of weakness of students with disabilities and be prepared to assist in this content area. Maccini and Hughes (2000) discussed the challenges that many students with disabilities and weak arithmetic foundations face in algebra. To address potential weaknesses, both general and special educators need to be prepared to collaborate and affect the learning outcomes of their students in mathematics while understanding their roles in collaboration, content, and learning strategies through professional development and other endeavors related to the changes in how mathematics is taught (Brownell et al. 2004, 2005; Laframboise et al. 2004; McLeskey and Ross 2004).

For many students with LD, most of their individualized education plans have some type of focus on the need for reading or writing (Lyon 1995; Sabornie and deBettencourt 2004). As you work on reading and sense-making skills, look for cues that students either don't understand the language or begin to misbehave (i.e., act out or withdraw) when the language becomes more difficult.

As stated, UDL principles (www.cast.org) are a crucial tool that teachers should implement to help students access the high school mathematics curriculum. UDL principles ensure that teachers have many ways to engage students and to represent the concept to try to compensate for areas of weaknesses and maximize areas of strength. UDL offers tools to support the success of students with disabilities in the general education setting. The concepts of UDL are simple (Rose and Meyer 2002) and successful; teachers both understand and apply these principles in every lesson all day long. The Center for Applied Special Technology (CAST) defines the following three core principles that teachers should consider when creating UDL-based instruction:

- Principle I: provide multiple means of representation (the "what" of learning)
- Principle II: provide multiple means of expression (the "how" of learning)
- Principle III: provide multiple means of engagement (the "why" of learning)

These three principles focus on creating a classroom that, much as the Americans with Disabilities Act ensured access to all buildings (e.g., adding ramps, elevators, and accessible drinking fountains), a UDL-based classroom gives all students access to the content. These principles ensure that all students can have multiple ways to access the Common Core Standards, express their understanding, and engage in the lesson. Embracing the UDL approach in the high school classroom parallels the intent of the *Reasoning and Sense Making* principles: that no longer can the purpose of high school mathematics be to just "sit and get" the Common Core; the purpose should be to build a community of scholars where the needs of students with disabilities are given access and equal opportunities to express and engage in the learning environment.

Moreover, using UDL principles helps to support students with cognitive delays or processing issues who might have trouble with higher-order questions. Given the value of higher-order thinking and questioning as the core of reasoning and sense making, researchers have identified several strategies, such as drill repetition, directed questioning, and sequencing, that have increased student achievement. Other examples—direct instruction (Ellis et al. 1991), mnemonic strategies (Brigham and Brigham 2001), graphic representations (Brigham, Scruggs, and Mastropieri 1995), strategy cues, mnemonics, controlling the difficulty or processing demands of a task, graphic organizers, and differentiated instruction—are also effective strategies for use with students with disabilities (Ellis et al. 1991; Fuchs and Fuchs 1995; Jitendra 2002).

This chapter is not meant to encompass all the research and literature on mathematics; however, we wanted to develop a thorough reference list on mathematics and major findings that relate to teaching students with disabilities at the secondary level (see table 3.2). As readers will note, the literature in high school mathematics for students with disabilities is sparse, but understanding the current research and embracing the idea that instruction may need to be adapted or modified for students with disabilities is a must for improving the overall outcome of mathematics performance schoolwide, statewide, and nationwide. Continuing to measure our success against that of countries that do not respect the educational needs of all students will be an ongoing struggle. Yet we also acknowledge the importance of giving students with disabilities the same opportunities as their nondisabled peers to gain access to advanced careers for which we know that mathematics is often a core skill.

Combining Teachers' Strengths and Minimizing Their Weaknesses through Collaboration

To maximize students' strengths and to minimize their weaknesses at the secondary level, special educators and mathematics educators must collaborate. This collaboration could be in the form of coteaching. Alternatively, special educators could work in more of a facilitative support or consultative role of offering suggestions to mathematics teachers through planning, assessing, or instruction; or they might even teach a section of mathematics that is a pretaught or foundational skill set for students. No matter the model, the key lies in tapping the expertise of mathematics teachers and special educators—and specific knowledge about students with needs—to ensure that all students can make sense of secondary mathematics.

In accordance with the movement to emphasize reasoning and sense making in teaching and learning mathematics, special educators need to recommend to mathematics teachers ways to ensure that students with disabilities have access to a structure for success. Mathematics and special education teachers should also combine their expertise to directly support areas of weakness for students with language or academic challenges (Magiera et al. 2005; Scruggs, Mastropieri, and McDuffie 2007). Conceptually, the general educator, as a mathematics teacher, has the necessary content knowledge, whereas the special educator knows how to accommodate, modify, and differentiate instruction and foster learning strategies. Both teachers bring essential knowledge about learning (Brownell, Hirsch, and Seo 2004; Brownell et al. 2005; Laframboise, Epanchin, and Colucci 2004; McLeskey and Ross 2004). Special educators' experience in teaching students with learning and behavioral disabilities can yield great ideas to improve teaching in general. These ideas often help students who may not have a disability but are struggling in the classroom.

The following example (from "Meaningful Words, Part A" on p. 74 of *Focus in High School Mathematics: Reasoning and Sense Making*) shows how two teachers can collaborate in one classroom. When a special educator enters the lesson as a coteacher, the teachers plan their roles and choose one or more types of coteaching (Dieker 2006; Dieker and Murawski 2003). Although several variations of coteaching exist, most include a general and special educator and coplanning, coinstruction, coassessment, and heterogeneous groups in a shared physical space (Friend and Cook 2003; Murawski and Dieker 2004; Murawski and Swanson 2001). Six types of coteaching exist: (1) one teacher teaches, one observes; (2) one teacher teaches, one leads; (3) station teaching; (4) parallel teaching; (5) alternative teaching; and (6) team teaching. Each model offers benefits to the learning environment (Friend and Cook 2004) that manifest when teachers work together directly. A new model, facilitative support, has emerged to support teachers in mathematics (Dieker 2009). In facilitative support, special educators help mathematics teachers with coplanning, coinstructing, or coassessing only. In this emerging role, the special educator supports too many classes to offer daily or direct support but can furnish support once or twice a week in targeted areas of need. No matter the support model, the fields of special education and mathematics need each other's expertise to really address the needs of all learners.

In our example we will assume that the special educator is not in a facilitative support role but instead is presenting direct instruction through the coteaching model. During planning, these teachers decided to use two types of coteaching, which are the ones observed most often in secondary mathematics classrooms: (1) one leads, one supports and (2) station teaching. During their fifty minutes of instruction, the special educator starts in the lead role. The special educator carries out a five-minute review/discussion activity on the lesson from yesterday, reviewing key vocabulary words (a strength of many special educators) and asking students to relate the mathematical terms from the previous day to at least two examples from their own lives. While the special educator leads, the general educator takes attendance, gathers homework, deals with any discipline or tardiness issues and then—before the end of the five minutes—does a sweep around each cooperative group, giving positive feedback on examples and correcting or discussing any potential misconceptions about the mathematical terms. (The strengths of a great cotaught classroom are that no downtime exists for students and that both teachers are constantly checking to ensure that all students are fully engaged.) While the students are talking, the special educator ensures that students are using and writing the correct mathematics vocabulary from what they learned yesterday.

After the five-minute review/opening activity, the general educator then introduces the lesson. She asks the same questions that he or she would normally ask in a classroom without students with special needs. Meanwhile, the special educator sweeps throughout the groups, encouraging students to participate and checking learning and behavioral goals on students' individualized education plans, ensuring that she is delivering in this mathematics class what is special about special education.

After the large-group discussion (as outlined on pp. 74–75 of *Focus in High School Mathematics: Reasoning and Sense Making*), the students are divided into two groups, both of which include students with various ability levels. One group (station-teaching model) looks at additional dot plots and further discusses the concepts in an even smaller group with the mathematics teacher (the content expert). The other group, led by the special educator, again discusses the language components to ensure that the students can apply terms to real life. Then this group will visit the National Virtual Manipulatives Library (nlvm.usu.edu/en/nav/vLibrary.html) and complete a coin-toss activity to further discuss mean, median, and mode, as well as to create their own data set to use in the large-group lesson the next day. After fifteen minutes, the groups switch, and each teacher repeats the activity with her second small group.

Seven minutes before the bell rings, the mathematics teacher asks the students to write a paragraph explaining what they learned in class today to serve as their exit ticket from class. The special educator gives students writing support as needed and reminds students to try to use the correct terminology and recall the many examples in their final written assignment today. At the end of the lesson, the two teachers split up the written paragraphs to review any misconceptions, giving the special educator a chance to look over the work of the students she is there to serve. Both teachers agree to review and meet for five minutes before school the next day to see whether they need to revise their plans to do another discussion with the groups before further analyzing their coin-toss data outcomes. The special educator agrees to find a good Brain Pop clip (www.brainpop.com) to use as a review for the lesson at the end of the week.

Although these two teachers might have different levels of mathematics expertise, they both have a strong foundation in ensuring that students make sense of the lesson. The crucial factor that occurred with these two teachers: the mathematics teacher was clear as to what she wanted students to learn, so the special educator could make it her goal to ensure that all students, including those with disabilities, learned what they needed to learn. Often, when true collaboration and meaningful (even limited, as it may be at the secondary level) planning exist, teams can work together to ensure that all students' strengths are maximized and weaknesses minimized—which truly makes sense in a class focused on high school mathematics students developing reasoning and sense-making skills.

Conclusion

Throughout this chapter, we have claimed that many of the goals for students without disabilities are appropriate for students with disabilities. Reasoning and sense making is a must for all students, and students with disabilities must have the opportunity to do so under conditions that not only challenge them but also give them the support mechanisms that they need for their particular disabilities. We presented examples of mechanisms, which often are reform based, such as using real-world problems, furnishing manipulatives that help students make sense of the mathematics, orchestrating meaningful discourse, and building on the knowledge that students bring with them into the classroom. We have also acknowledged that the mathematics educator and the special-needs educator should work together, using each other's strengths to maximize the mathematics potential of all students.

Table 3.2
Selected current research on secondary special education and mathematics

Reference	Special-Educational Approach						
	Explicit instruction	Inquiry instruction	Visual enhancements	Instructional examples	Problem solving	Peer assistance	Verbalization and metacognition
Baker, Gersten, and Lee (2002)	Explicit instruction produced consistent positive results.	Contextualized instruction led to increased transfer of mathematical concepts; effectiveness for students who struggled inconclusive.					
Baxter, Woodward, and Olson (2001)	Complexity of some reform-based curricula (e.g., multiple concepts taught at once) was troublesome for students with LD; explicit sequencing beneficial.	Low achievers may need additional supports in large-group inquiry/standards-based mathematics classrooms.				Students moving back and forth between roles of tutor and tutee in sessions effective for students with LD.	
Baxter et al. (2002)		A summary of strategies used is needed. Use small-group mini-lessons over effective strategies. Review problems.					
Bottge et al. (2002)				Prompts should be built into the general education curriculum.			
Butler et al. (2003)			Include all levels of the concrete–representational–abstract (CRA) process to enhance conceptual meaning; CRA more effective than RA alone.	Varying the range of examples used during instruction aids student understanding.			

Table 3.2—*Continued*
Selected current research on secondary special education and mathematics

Reference	Special-Educational Approach						
	Explicit instruction	Inquiry instruction	Visual enhancements	Instructional examples	Problem solving	Peer assistance	Verbalization and metacognition
Griffin and Jitendra (2009)					Schema-based problem solving benefited students more than general strategy instruction. Strategy should be revisited often.		
Griffin, Jitendra, and League (2009)	"Explicitness" strengthens student understanding of the mathematics from teacher press and heavy questioning; intense teacher–student interactions.		Hands-on materials demonstrate abstract concepts and visual representations, improving understanding of math concepts.				Teacher press ("why" and "how" questions) elicits a degree of student involvement to facilitate explicit reasoning.
Ives and Hoy (2003)			Augmenting direct strategy instruction with graphic organizers improved performance on several achievement measures.				
Jayanthi, Gersten, and Baker (2008)	Modeling and thinking aloud during presentation of new material aids in understanding.		Students and teachers must use visuals during instruction for students to benefit. Students with disabilities work better with teacher-supplied visuals than with self-generated visuals.	Focus and sequencing of instructional examples is essential in initial understanding of concepts; range of examples vital for transfer of mathematical understanding to new situations. Multiple-strategy instruction can take the form of a heuristic and facilitate discourse.		Assistance from older students to younger students has proven more effective than same-age peer tutoring.	Verbalization of mathematical thinking helps manage the impulsive characteristics exhibited by students with disabilities during problem solving and aids in student understanding of procedural steps.

Table 3.2—*Continued*
Selected current research on secondary special education and mathematics

Reference	Special-Educational Approach						
	Explicit instruction	Inquiry instruction	Visual enhancements	Instructional examples	Problem solving	Peer assistance	Verbalization and metacognition
Kroesbergen and van Luit (2002)		Small-group instruction more beneficial in this type of instruction for children. Students with mild disabilities appeared to learn just as well from realistic mathematics as their peers.					
Kroesbergen, van Luit, and Maas (2004)	Self-instruction and direct instruction effective for teaching students with LD. Low achievers do not always need explicit instruction. Explicit instruction beneficial to teach a small group strategies.	Constructivist teaching benefited students more than traditional instruction, but not as much as explicit instruction. Smaller instructional groups benefited all types of instruction.				Peer tutoring sometimes effective but not as effective as intensive interactions with teachers.	
Kunsch, Jitendra, and Sood (2007)				Students who used schema-based instruction did better on problem-solving tasks than those who were taught general problem-solving strategies.			

Table 3.2—*Continued*
Selected current research on secondary special education and mathematics

Reference	Special-Educational Approach						
	Explicit instruction	Inquiry instruction	Visual enhancements	Instructional examples	Problem solving	Peer assistance	Verbalization and metacognition
Montague (2007)				Checklists and strategy steps can be incorporated into a problem-solving system for students with LD to present their thoughts in the open and make the process more explicit.			Metacognition helps students improve their attempts to understand the problem, their use of strategies, and how they formulate solutions.
National Mathematics Advisory Panel (2008)	Students should work in small groups or pairs with close interaction with the teacher to learn to solve several problems with different characteristics.						
Rittle-Johnson and Star (2007)	Students should work in small groups or pairs with close interaction with the teacher to learn to solve several problems with different characteristics.			Discussion of various solution strategies promoted greater thinking in mathematics (algebra) than listening to one solution strategy at a time.			
Scheuermann, Deshler, and Schumaker (2009)	Sequencing of instruction into small steps is explicitly done during planning of instruction.	Inquiry should be scaffolded and carefully sequenced. Representation and processing for students with LD is increased with this form of inquiry.					

Table 3.2—*Continued*
Selected current research on secondary special education and mathematics

Reference	Special-Educational Approach						
	Explicit instruction	Inquiry instruction	Visual enhancements	Instructional examples	Problem solving	Peer assistance	Verbalization and metacognition
Van Garderen and Montague (2003)					Students with LD tend to need support in generating schematic representations for problem solving.		
Witzel, Mercer, and Miller (2003)			CRA sequence is more effective than abstract-only instruction for teaching mathematics to LD students.				
Woodward (2006)				Students should be taught to solve problems by using multiple strategies and should compare and contrast strategies learned.			
Xin, Jitendra, and Deatline-Buchman (2005)			Visuals to support the understanding of a particular problem type are effective in teaching students with LD to understand concepts and translate words into equations.				

References

Access Center. *Using Peer Tutoring to Facilitate Access*. Washington, D.C.: Access Center, 2004.

Allsopp, David H. "Using Classwide Peer Tutoring to Teach Beginning Algebra Problem-Solving Skills in Heterogeneous Classrooms." *Remedial and Special Education* 18 (November–December 1997): 367–79.

Allsopp, David, Louann Lovin, Gerald Green, and Emma Savage-Davis. "Why Students with Special Needs Have Difficulty Learning Mathematics and What Teachers Can Do to Help." *Mathematics Teaching in the Middle School* 8 (February 2003): 308–14.

Baker, Scott, Russell Gersten, and Dae-Sik Lee. "A Synthesis of Empirical Research on Teaching Mathematics to Low-Achieving Students." *Elementary School Journal* 103 (September 2002): 51–73.

Baxter, Juliet, John Woodward, and Deborah Olson. "Effects of Reform-Based Mathematics Instruction on Low Achievers in Five Third-Grade Classrooms." *Elementary School Journal* 101 (May 2001): 529–47.

Baxter, Juliet, John Woodward, Jill Voorhies, and Jennifer Wong. "We Talk about It, but Do They Get It?" *Learning Disabilities Research and Practice* 17 (August 2002): 173–85.

Bottge, Brian, Mary Heinrichs, Shih-Yi Chan, and Ronald Serlin. "Anchoring Adolescents' Understanding of Math Concepts in Rich Problem-Solving Environments." *Remedial and Special Education* 22 (September–October 2001): 299–314.

Bottge, Brian A., Mary Heinrichs, Zara D. Mehta, and Ya-Hui Hung. "Weighing the Benefits of Anchored Instruction for Students with Disabilities in General Education Classes." *Journal of Special Education* 35 (Winter 2002): 186–200.

Bottge, Brian A., Enrique Rueda, Perry T. LaRoque, Ronald C. Serlin, and Jung Min Kwon. "Integrating Reform-Oriented Math Instruction in Special Education Settings." *Learning Disabilities Research and Practice* 22 (May 2007): 96–109.

Bottge, Brian A., Enrique Rueda, Ronald C. Serlin, Ya-Hui Hung, and Jung Min Kwon. "Shrinking Achievement Differences with Anchored Math Problems: Challenges and Possibilities." *Journal of Special Education* 41 (Spring 2007): 31–49.

Bottge, Brian, Enrique Rueda, and Michael Skivington. "Situating Math Instruction in Rich Problem-Solving Contexts: Effects on Adolescents with Challenging Behaviors." *Behavioral Disorders* 31 (August 2006): 394–407.

Brigham, Richard, and Michelle Brigham. "A Focus on Mnemonic Instruction." *Current Practice Alerts* (issue 5; Summer 2001): 1–4. www.teachingld.org/pdf/Alert5.pdf (accessed August 23, 2010).

Brigham, Frederick J., Thomas E. Scruggs, and Margo A. Mastropieri. "Elaborative Maps for Enhanced Learning of Historical Information: Uniting Spatial, Verbal, and Imaginal Information." *Journal of Special Education* 28 (Winter 1995): 440–60.

Brownell, Mary T., Eric Hirsch, and Seonjin Seo. "Meeting the Demand for Highly Qualified Special Education Teachers during Severe Shortages: What Should Policymakers Consider?" *Journal of Special Education* 38 (March 2004): 56–61.

Brownell, Mary T., Doreen D. Ross, Elayne P. Colon, and Cynthia L. McCallum. "Critical Features of Special Education Teacher Preparation: A Comparison with General Teacher Education." *Journal of Special Education* 38 (Winter 2005): 242–52.

Butler, Francis, Susan P. Miller, Kevin Crehan, Beatrice Babbitt, and Thomas Pierce. "Fraction Instruction for Students with Mathematics Disabilities: Comparing Two Teaching Sequences." *Learning Disabilities Research and Practice* 18 (May 2003): 99–111.

Callahan, Rebecca M. "Tracking and High School English Learners: Limiting Opportunity to Learn." *American Educational Research Journal* 42 (Summer 2005): 305–28.

Center for Implementing Technology in Education (CITEd). "Beyond 'Getting the Answer': Calculators Help Learning-Disabled Students Get the Concepts." 2007. www.ldonline.org/article/19274 (accessed August 23, 2010).

Data Accountability Center. "Part B Data and Notes. IDEA 618 Data Tables: Educational Environment." 2007. www.ideadata.org/PartBData.asp (accessed August 23, 2010).

Dieker, Lisa A. *The Co-Teaching Lesson Plan Book*. Whitefish Bay, Wis.: Knowledge by Design, 2006.

———. "Strategies for Co-Teaching and Inclusive Practices." Paper presented at the University of Central Florida, College of Education, Orlando, Fla., 2009.

Dieker, Lisa A., and Craig A. Berg. "Collaborative Program Development Between Secondary Science, Mathematics and Special Educators." *Teacher Education and Special Education* 25 (January 2002): 92–99.

Dieker, Lisa A., and Wendy W. Murawski. "Co-Teaching at the Secondary Level: Unique Issues, Current Trends, and Suggestions for Success." *High School Journal* 86 (April–May 2003): 1–13.

Ellis, Edwin S., Donald Deshler, Jean B. Schumaker, and F. Clark. "An Instructional Model for Teaching Learning Strategies." *Focus on Exceptional Children* 23 (February 1991): 1–24.

Friend, Marilyn, and Lynne Cook. *Interactions: Collaboration Skills for School Professionals*. Boston: Allyn and Bacon, 2003.

Fuchs, Douglas, and Lynn S. Fuchs. "What's 'Special' about Special Education? A Field under Siege." *Phi Delta Kappan* 76, no. 7 (1995): 522–30.

Griffin, Cynthia C., and Asha K. Jitendra. "Word Problem Solving in Inclusive Third-Grade Mathematics Classrooms." *Journal of Educational Research* 102 (January–February 2009): 187–201.

Griffin, Cynthia C., Asha K. Jitendra, and Martha B. League. "Novice Special Educators' Instructional Practices, Communication Patterns, and Content Knowledge for Teaching Mathematics." *Teacher Education and Special Education* 32, no. 4 (2009): 319–36.

Heward, William L. "Ten Faulty Notions about Teaching and Learning that Hinder the Effectiveness of Special Education." *Journal of Special Education* 36 (Winter 2003): 186–205.

Ives, Bob. "Graphic Organizers Applied to Secondary Algebra Instruction for Students with Learning Disorders." *Learning Disabilities Research and Practice* 22 (May 2007): 110–18.

Ives, Bob, and Cheri C. Hoy. "Graphic Organizers Applied to Higher-Level Secondary Mathematics." *Learning Disabilities Research and Practice* 18 (February 2003): 36–51.

Jayanthi, Madhavi, Russell Gersten, and Scott Baker. *Mathematics Instruction for Students with Learning Disabilities or Difficulty Learning Mathematics: A Guide for Teachers*. Portsmouth, N.H.: RMC Research Corp., Center on Instruction, 2008.

Jitendra, Asha. "Teaching Students Math Problem-Solving through Graphic Representations." *Teaching Exceptional Children* 34 (March–April 2002): 34–38.

Kroesbergen, Evelyn H., and Johannes van Luit. "Teaching Multiplication to Low Math Performers: Guided versus Structured Instruction." *Instructional Science* 30 (September 2002): 361–78.

Kroesbergen, Evelyn H., Johannes van Luit, and Cora J. M. Maas. "Effectiveness of Explicit and Constructivist Mathematics Instruction for Low-Achieving Students in the Netherlands." *Elementary School Journal* 104 (January 2004): 233–51.

Kunsch, Catherine A., Asha K. Jitendra, and Sheetal Sood. "The Effects of Peer-Mediated Instruction in Mathematics for Students with Learning Problems: A Research Synthesis." *Learning Disabilities Research and Practice* 22 (February 2007): 1–12.

Laframboise, Kathy, Betty Epanchin, and Karen Colucci. "Working Together: Emerging Roles of Special and General Education Teachers in Inclusive Settings." *Action in Teacher Education* 26, no. 3 (2004): 29–43.

Lyon, G. Reid. "Reading Initiatives in LD: Contributions from Scientists Supported by the National Institute of Child Health and Development." *Journal of Child Neurology* 10 (Suppl. 1 1995): S120–26.

Maccini, Paula, and Charles Hughes. "Effects of a Problem-Solving Strategy on the Introductory Algebra Performance of Secondary Students with Learning Disabilities." *Learning Disabilities Research and Practice* 15 (Winter 2000): 10–21.

Maccini, Paula, Candice A. Mulcahy, and Michael G. Wilson. "A Follow-Up of Mathematics Interventions for Secondary Students with Learning Disabilities." *Learning Disabilities Research and Practice* 22 (February 2007): 58–74.

Maccini, Paula, and Kathy L. Ruhl. "Effects of Graduated Instructional Sequence on the Algebraic Subtraction of Integers by Secondary Students with Learning Disabilities." *Education and Treatment of Children* 23 (November 2000): 465–89.

Maccini, Paula, Tricia Strickland, Joseph C. Gagnon, and Kimber Malmgren. "Accessing the General Education Math Curriculum for Secondary Students with High-Incidence Disabilities." *Focus on Exceptional Children* 40 (April 2008): 1–32.

Magiera, Kathleen, Cynthia Smith, Naomi Zigmond, and Kelli Gebauer. "Benefits of Co-Teaching in Secondary Mathematics Classes." *Teaching Exceptional Children* 37 (January–February 2005): 20–24.

McLaughlin, Margaret J., and Martha Thurlow. "Educational Accountability and Students with Disabilities: Issues and Challenges." *Educational Policy* 17 (September 2003): 431–51.

McLeskey, James, and Doreen D. Ross. "The Politics of Teacher Education in the New Millennium: Implications for Special Education Teacher Educators." *Teacher Education and Special Education* 27 (October 2004): 342–49.

Montague, Marjorie. "Self-Regulation and Mathematics Instruction." *Learning Disabilities Research and Practice* 22 (February 2007): 75–83.

Murawski, Wendy W., and Lisa A. Dieker. "Tips and Strategies for Co-Teaching at the Secondary Level." *Teaching Exceptional Children* 36, no. 5 (2004): 52–58.

National Council of Teachers of Mathematics (NCTM). *Curriculum Focal Points for Prekindergarten through Grade 8 Mathematics: A Quest for Coherence.* Reston, Va.: NCTM, 2006.

———. "Equity in Mathematics Education." January 2008. www.nctm.org/about/content.aspx?id=13490 (accessed September 12, 2010).

———. *Focus in High School Mathematics: Reasoning and Sense Making.* Reston, Va.: NCTM, 2009.

National Mathematics Advisory Panel. *Foundations for Success: The Final Report of the National Mathematics Advisory Panel.* Washington, D.C.: U.S. Department of Education, 2008.

Rittle-Johnson, Bethany, and Jon R. Star. "Does Comparing Solution Methods Facilitate Conceptual and Procedural Knowledge? An Experimental Study on Learning to Solve Equations." *Journal of Educational Psychology* 99 (August 2007): 561–74.

Rose, David, and Anne Meyer. *Teaching Every Student in the Digital Age: Universal Design for Learning.* Alexandria, Va.: ASCD, 2002.

Sabornie, Edward J., and Laurie U. deBettencourt. *Teaching Students with Mild and High-Incidence Disabilities at the Secondary Level.* 2nd ed. Upper Saddle River, N.J.: Pearson, 2004.

Scheuermann, Amy M., Donald D. Deshler, and Jean B. Schumaker. "The Effects of the Explicit Inquiry Routine on the Performance of Students with Learning Disabilities on One-Variable Equations." *Learning Disability Quarterly* 32 (Spring 2009): 103–20.

Scruggs, Thomas E., Margo A. Mastropieri, and Kimberly A. McDuffie. "Co-Teaching in Inclusive Classrooms: A Metasynthesis of Qualitative Research." *Exceptional Children* 73 (Summer 2007): 392–416.

Strickland, Tricia K., and Paula Maccini. "Teaching Algebra to Students with Learning Disabilities: Follow-Up Review of the Literature." *Intervention in School and Clinic* 46 (September 2010): 38–45.

U.S. Department of Education. No Child Left Behind Act. Washington, D.C.: U.S. Department of Education, 2001.

———. Individuals with Disabilities Education Improvement Act (IDEIA). Washington, D.C.: U.S. Department of Education, 2004.

van Garderen, Delinda, and Marjorie Montague. "Visual–Spatial Representation, Mathematical Problem Solving, and Students of Varying Abilities." *Learning Disabilities Research and Practice* 18 (November 2003): 246–54.

Wehby, Joseph H., Kathleen L. Lane, and Katherine B. Falk. "Academic Instruction for Students with Emotional and Behavioral Disorders." *Journal of Emotional and Behavioral Disorders* 11 (Winter 2003): 194–97.

Witzel, Bradley S., Cecil D. Mercer, and M. David Miller. "Teaching Algebra to Students with Learning Difficulties: An Investigation of an Explicit Instruction Model." *Learning Disabilities Research and Practice* 18 (May 2003): 121–31.

Woodward, John. "Making Reform-Based Mathematics Work for Academically Low-Achieving Middle School Students." In *Teaching Mathematics to Middle School Students with Learning Difficulties*, edited by Marjorie Montague and Asha Jitendra, pp. 29–50. New York: Guilford Press, 2006.

Xin, Yan P., Asha K. Jitendra, and Andria Deatline-Buchman. "Effects of Mathematical Word Problem–Solving Instruction on Middle School Students with Learning Problems." *Journal of Special Education* 39 (Fall 2005): 181–92.

Chapter 4

Issues of Equity for Advanced Students

Tamar Avineri, Christine Belledin, Julie Graves, Richard Noble,
Maria Hernandez, Donita Robinson, and Dan Teague

The Equity Principle in *Principles and Standards for School Mathematics* (National Council of Teachers of Mathematics [NCTM] 2000) requires that teachers and schools attend to the needs of all students, "regardless of their personal characteristics, backgrounds, or physical challenges" (p. 12). To accomplish this objective, NCTM insists on the provision of higher expectations and worthwhile opportunities while accommodating student differences with resources and support.

The Equity Principle does not state that every student should receive the same instruction. Equity demands a respect for individual differences in readiness to learn and recognizes the value and needs of each student. Equity ensures that all students have access to a coherent, challenging mathematics curriculum taught by capable, caring, and well-supported teachers. The appropriate level of challenge, the exploratory and creative manner in which students are brought to surmount those challenges, and how student progress is assessed are crucial features of instruction for high-ability, high-interest students.

Discussions of educational equity often focus on certain populations of students—those who are impoverished, those who speak English as a second language, those with disabilities, or those who are nonwhite (NCTM 2000). However, students with special capabilities, such as high ability and high interest in mathematics—which includes members from all the populations previously mentioned—often get less attention. Although the educational needs of students with strong interest and abilities in mathematics are in some ways unique, Saul noted, "The basic principles of good teaching transfer over to work with high-ability students" (1999, p. 83). Similarly, many methods of instruction essential to developing high-ability students are also appropriate for all students.

Who Is an Advanced Student in Mathematics?

As many criteria for determining who is advanced exist as there are descriptors of such students (e.g., gifted, honors, highly talented, advanced, precocious). All these descriptors recognize that a student doesn't have to be a child prodigy or competing for a place on the U.S.A. Mathematical Olympiad team to be considered talented and interested in mathematics, and these students should be taught accordingly. For this chapter, we take Renzulli's (1984) depiction of giftedness as our working definition. For Renzulli, a gifted mathematics student is one who (1) shows above-average general ability; (2) has a strong commitment to mathematics; and (3) can offer creative solutions to nonstandard problems when given the opportunity. Every high school has gifted students, though the traditional methods and standardized tests may not identify them as such. Without properly motivating, encouraging, and intellectually challenging gifted students, we may lose some of their mathematical talents forever.

Most states have criteria for identifying gifted students and recognize the need for appropriate courses to develop these students' talent. North Carolina recognizes the different needs of students across the educational spectrum and requires equity in education with respect to their special needs in its legislation on schools and schooling: "Academically or intellectually gifted students exhibit high performance capability in intellectual areas, specific academic fields, or in both intellectual areas and specific academic fields. Academically or intellectually gifted students require differentiated educational services beyond those that the regular educational program ordinarily offers. Outstanding abilities are present in students from all cultural groups, across all economic strata, and in all areas of human endeavor" (North Carolina Gen. Stat. § 115C–150.5).

Forty-five other states have similar legislation. So, what's the problem? Don't the top kids always get the best teachers, the best curriculum, and the most attention?

The Problem Facing Advanced Students

Every few years, a new study reports on the challenges that the United States faces from overseas competition and stresses the need for improved performance and more students' going into science, technology, engineering, and mathematics fields and other mathematics-intensive disciplines. Each new report echoes the warning from "An Agenda for Action": "The most neglected, in terms of realizing full potential, is the gifted student of mathematics. Outstanding mathematical ability is a precious societal resource, sorely needed to maintain leadership in a technological world" (NCTM 1980). With each new decade's report issuing the same challenge, it seems that not enough has been done since 1980 to capture the interest of and fully develop the special talents of this "precious societal resource," our talented students of mathematics.

More recently, the *NCTM Task Force Report on Promising Students* recommended, "New curricular standards, programs, and materials should be developed to encourage and challenge the development of promising mathematical students" (Bennett et al. 1999). The University of Iowa report *A Nation Deceived: How Schools Hold Back Our Brightest Students* reiterates this call for a curriculum that accounts for advanced students' special needs: "These gifted students come in with a different attitude, and that attitude must be honored with a challenging curriculum. If that different curriculum is not provided, teenage ambition can easily turn into boredom and a lifetime of missed opportunities" (Colangelo, Assouline, and Gross 2004, p. 29).

The high school years offer a brief opportunity in which we can engage and cultivate each student's talents. Yet for many advanced students, classroom experiences in mathematics offer insufficient appeal, and they turn to other areas of interest that are more attuned to their need for creative and stimulating engagement (Colangelo, Assouline, and Gross 2004). Recent budget cuts coupled with testing programs focused on minimum standards may reduce schools' abilities to focus energy on the needs of highly able students. The No Child Left Behind (NCLB) legislation has exacerbated problems in this area. Goodkin (2005) noted, "By forcing schools to focus their time and funding almost entirely on bringing low-achieving students up to proficiency, NCLB sacrifices the education of the gifted students who will become our future biomedical researchers, computer engineers, and other scientific leaders."

Further support for these findings comes from the 2008 Fordham Institute report *High-Achieving Students in the Era of NCLB* (Duffett, Farkas, and Loveless 2008) and the National Association of Gifted Education in its 2008–2009 *State of the Nation in Gifted Education* report. The latter concludes that "there is a markedly insufficient national commitment to gifted and talented children, which, if left unchecked, will ultimately leave our nation ill-prepared to field the next generation of innovators and to compete in the global economy" (NAGC 2009, p. 2).

Many may argue that, in these times of diminished resources for education, the advanced students are the most able to fend for themselves and the least damaged by neglect. Although many advanced students will meet minimal requirements without significant teacher input, such benign neglect fails to ensure equity and ultimately results in a huge cumulative loss in intellectual capital for the country.

Potential Dangers on the Road to AP Calculus

In "Meeting the Educational Needs of Special Populations," Vanderbilt researchers argue that "intellectually talented students are an extraordinary national resource, and much research supports the importance of providing them with specialized learning environments to meet their unique intellectual and socio-emotional needs" (Bleske-Rechek, Lubinski, and Benbow 2004, p. 217). They also suggest that the Advanced Placement (AP) program affords one such learning environment (Stanley and Benbow 1982).

More and more students are taking AP calculus each year; is this evidence that teachers are addressing the needs of the advanced students? AP calculus should certainly be a part of advanced students' high school mathematical experience, but we argue that it should not be the totality. The AP program in mathematics, by itself, does not fully address the mathematical needs of advanced students. AP courses are not designed to serve as honors-level college courses but rather to parallel the standard freshman-level college courses. Consequently, AP calculus is not designed specifically to meet the needs and interests of students with special talent in mathematics, nor has it the explicit goal of developing student interest in mathematics by offering high-level investigative experiences emphasizing the creative aspects of mathematical discovery. The large and increasing number of advanced high school students for whom AP calculus is their last mathematics experience attests to this truth.

The National Research Council (2002) report *Learning and Understanding: Improving Advanced Study of Mathematics and Science in American High Schools* describes the limitations of the AP calculus curriculum for advanced high school students: "Particularly able AP students could profit from an AP course enriched by modeling activities and more attention to proof. In this sense, AP calculus is seen as a minimal course for advanced study rather than a maximal course" (p. 509).

Dan Kennedy, former chair of the AP Calculus Test Development Committee, described one unintended consequence of the AP program. His presentation at the NCTM annual meeting in April 2005 raised the question of the role of discovery in the AP program:

> There was never enough time in AP science courses to allow for discovery; now there is not enough time in the *entire curriculum* for discovery, since the students are being rushed into more and more AP courses by the bean-counters. . . . AP calculus has the same limiting effect on the curriculum. When you get right down to it, the pre-calculus rope comprises a surprisingly small number of algebraic and geometric strands, especially if you know you are preparing specifically for AB Calculus, which does not involve vectors, infinite series, or polar coordinates. Topics like statistics, probability, matrices, mathematical induction, graph theory, linear programming, and even financial topics like amortization and mortgages that will affect almost every student someday, are given short shrift in the core curriculum precisely because they are not necessary for studying calculus.

The explosive growth in AP calculus has unintentionally limited the opportunity for many students to explore any mathematics that is not explicitly a prerequisite for AP calculus. Limiting the prerequisite material to just that needed for calculus allows many more students to study calculus in high school, but to what end and to what advantage for those students?

Block-scheduled preparatory work, in which a full year's material is compressed into one semester, can exacerbate the deleterious effects of a narrow focus on preparing for calculus. The combination of shortened exposure and shortsighted AP preparation can significantly alter students' perceptions of mathematics and limit their ability and desire to move forward in mathematics once they have completed calculus. These students can exit our mathematical pipeline advanced in the listing of courses taken but deficient in the breadth of their background and the depth of their mathematical experiences.

Reasoning and Sense Making for All

America's future certainly depends on the mathematical capabilities of all our students, and "mathematics for all" has been a primary focus of curriculum development that the National Science Foundation has funded and that NCTM programs have supported. America's future also depends on fully using the mathematical capabilities of our most talented students. Only curriculum and classroom experiences rooted in reasoning and sense making will allow the future professional users of mathematics to reach their full potential.

Ross, in the *Second Report of the MAA Task Force on the NCTM Standards*, said, "The foundation of mathematics is reasoning. . . . If reasoning ability is not developed in the student, then mathematics simply becomes a matter of following a set of procedures and mimicking examples without thought as to why they make sense" (MAA 1997). The American Mathematical Society Association Resource Group, which Roger Howe chaired, added, "The most important thing to emphasize about mathematical reasoning is that it exists—more, that it is the heart of the subject, that mathematics is a coherent subject, and that mathematical reasoning is what makes it so. . . . Mathematics should simply be taught as a subject where things make sense and where you can figure out why they are the way they are" (AMS 1997, p. 276).

Rewriting the Rules of the Game of Teaching and Learning

Assessing True Academic Success: The Next Frontier of Reform also has a wonderful exposition of the classical assessment in mathematics:

> The rules of that game are simple: we, the teachers show them what to do and how to do it; we let them practice at it for a while, and then we give them a test to see how closely they can match what we did. What we contribute to this game is called "teaching," what they contribute is called "learning," and the game is won or lost for both of us on test day. Ironically, thinking is not only absent from this process, but in a curious way actually counterproductive to the goals of the game.

> Thinking takes time. Thinking comes into play precisely when you cannot do something "without thinking." You can do something without thinking if you really know how to do it well. If your students can do something really well, then they have been very well prepared. Therefore, if both you and your students have done your jobs perfectly, they will proceed through your test without thinking. If you want your students to think on your test, then you will have to give them a question for which they have not been fully prepared. If they succeed, fine; in the more likely event that they do not, then they will rightfully complain about not being fully prepared. You and the student will have both failed to uphold your respective ends of the contract that your test was designed to validate, because thinking will have gotten in the way of the game. (Kennedy 1999, pp. 462–63)

Despite the efforts of NCTM and many other interested communities over the past decade, too many American students are exposed to this form of "the learning game." Such an approach is antithetical to developing reasoning and sense making and to developing mathematical creativity that expands student interest in mathematics.

Assessing student growth must be a carefully considered and integral part of instruction. Teachers who are expecting 90 percent proficiency from beginners cannot be asking much of importance or giving students real and significant challenges. Teachers should design assignments to draw insight, creative thought, and determined effort from the students. Students need assignments that allow extended time, encourage collaboration and animated discussion with student colleagues, and require consistent and sustained effort. Students need time to think deeply about a problem, move away from it, and return to reconsider the problem.

Schoenfeld (1988, p. 151) contended that steady exposure to instruction and assessment such as that described in "the learning game" leads to a belief system that hinders student growth and can result in the following student beliefs about mathematics and themselves as learners of mathematics.

- *Belief 1:* The processes of formal mathematics (e.g., "proof") have little or nothing to do with discovery or invention.

- *Belief 2:* Students who understand the subject matter can solve assigned mathematics problems in five minutes or less. Corollary: students stop working on a problem after just a few minutes since, if they haven't solved it, they didn't understand the material (and therefore will not solve it).

- *Belief 3:* Only geniuses can discover, create, or really understand mathematics. Corollary: mathematics is studied passively, with students accepting what is passed down "from above" without the expectation that they can make sense of it for themselves.

- *Belief 4:* One succeeds in school by performing the tasks, to the letter, as the teacher describes.

Many students who now are underserved would blossom in a challenging curriculum designed to expand and deepen their understanding of mathematics by engaging them in the exploratory enterprise and creativity of mathematical reasoning. This endeavor requires a curriculum, classroom atmosphere, and mode of instruction that has at its core reasoning and sense making.

Students' classroom experience must be active, thought provoking, and challenging. This means that the classroom experience will also challenge the teacher. Active classrooms with intrigued students require an alert and engaged method of instruction. The assignments and problems posed to the students are essential to provoking the appropriate student responses. Schoenfeld (2004) described it in this way:

> [Teaching with an exploratory approach] calls for both knowledge and flexibility on the part of the teacher, who must provide support for students as they engage in mathematical sense making. This means knowing mathematics well, having a sense of when to let students explore and when to tell them what they need to know, and knowing how to nudge them in productive directions. . . . Structuring and supervising student interactions so that students can make progress on the problems, learn from each other, and know when they need more expert advice is very hard. When these things are done well, students can learn a great deal. (p. 272)

The Importance of Struggle and Appropriate Mathematical Experiences

In *They're Not Dumb, They're Different: Stalking the Second Tier*, Tobias (1990) described the classroom experiences of strong students who were broadly capable and who, overwhelmingly, chose not to pursue mathematics and other science, technology, engineering, and mathematics disciplines as career options. She wanted to know why we lose them and their contributions from our disciplines. Although each student's reasons were individual and personal, they had a strong, persistent feature. One student described mathematical experiences with the following sentiment: "In social science, we read an article, and the teacher wants to know what we think about it. In math, the teacher never wants to know what we think, only if we remember what Descartes or some other mathematician thought." One way of describing this student's sentiment is to say, *We want to be in courses where we get to use our own minds.* Encouraging students to use their own minds is essential when working with students who are talented and interested in mathematics.

Saul's many years of experience with high-ability students convince him that "high-ability students who have no trouble with mathematics homework are understimulated and will soon turn their eager minds to other subjects. The need to be challenged is central to high-ability students" (1999, p. 83). As Saul (1999) pointed out, students must be working on problems that are rich enough to allow for extended work on them and sufficiently interesting and engaging so that they are willing to give the problems their time and intellectual energy. Short, five-minute problems don't generally lead to innovative solutions or deep understanding.

Here is an example of a rich problem:

Early in the season, Pat was hitting fewer than 80% of her free throws. At the end of the season, she was hitting more than 80% of her free throws.

(a) Must there have been a time during the season at which she was hitting exactly 80% of her free throws? If so, explain why. If not, give a counterexample.

(b) If the answer to (a) was yes, find all other values p that have this intermediate-value property (you can't go from below p to above p without going through exactly p). If the answer to (a) was no, are there any values of p for which this intermediate-value property does hold? If not, explain why there can be no such values.

Students who have studied the intermediate-value theorem will almost universally say that passing through 80 percent is not necessary because the problem is discrete rather than continuous. As they search for a counterexample, they find that every example they try indeed hits 80 percent. After a while, they try to understand why this is true and to find other values that have the same intermediate-value characteristics and to generalize the result. The teacher must allow students to think independently and creatively rather than guiding them to a solution. Here is how a teacher could, without giving too much direction, help students who are struggling with the problem.

Student A: We think that it's true that Pat's average had to be 80 percent at some point in the season, but we don't know why.

Teacher: Tell me what you have investigated so far.

Student B: We got stuck on figuring out why 80 percent has this property, so we decided to try other percentages. We found that 75 percent has the property, too, but 76 percent through 79 percent don't.

Student A: We also noticed that both the percentages we found to have the property can be written as simple fractions. We can write 0.80 as 4/5 and 0.75 as 3/4.

Teacher: Interesting! Tell me more about what you mean when you say that a fraction is "simple."

Student A: We mean that the fraction can be reduced to something like 4/5.

Teacher: Let's try to be more specific. Consider 78/100. It can be reduced to 39/50. Is that a simple fraction?

Student B: Well, no. And we know that the intermediate-value property doesn't hold for 78 percent.

Teacher: So it looks like you've noticed something about the two percentages you have found that have this intermediate-value theorem, but you have to think more carefully about what makes them different from the percentages that don't have the property. What could you do next to help clarify this?

The students will find in the end that one can write the common characteristic of percentages with this intermediate-value property as a rational number where the numerator is one less than the denominator. In the preceding exchange, the teacher helped the students identify the gap in their work and allowed them to use this insight to define their own path toward a solution.

The Paradox of the Student Mindset

With all the evidence pointing to high-talent students' desire for stimulating and challenging work, finding that many may initially resist such work seems paradoxical. Dweck (2006) has studied this phenomenon and divides students into two major classifications: those with a "fixed mindset" and those with a "growth mindset." Students with the fixed mindset have *performance goals* and believe that intelligence is fixed from birth and that effort cannot change their level of intelligence. Students with the growth mindset have *learning goals* and believe that one can develop intelligence and abilities through effort and active engagement.

In an interview for the online *Stanford Magazine* (Krakovsky 2007), Dweck summarizes, "Students for whom performance is paramount want to look smart even if it means not learning a thing in the process. For them, each task is a challenge to their self-image, and each setback becomes a personal threat. So they pursue only activities at which they're sure to shine. . . . Students with learning goals, on the other hand, take necessary risks and don't worry about failure because each mistake becomes a chance to learn" (p. 2). Novel and challenging problems give students with the growth mindset new opportunities to grow, whereas for those with the fixed mindset, they offer only an opportunity to be seen as a fraud.

Our experience suggests that a significant number of students come into advanced courses with this fixed mindset and resent mightily the teacher's efforts to draw original and creative work from them. Students view as unfair being asked to create a solution to a problem that they have not explicitly been taught to solve because it threatens their image of being talented. If these students are to develop their natural creativity, the teacher must first revise the students' (and often the parents') view of mathematics and challenge their ability in new ways.

The good news, as Dweck (2006) points out, is that a student's mindset can change. If students are to change their mindsets about learning mathematics, they must be given carefully selected problems that draw them into a conversation and show them the joy of true and developmentally appropriate mathematical investigation. Helping advanced students develop a growth mindset is particularly important so that they can take full advantage of their academic talents and potential.

The midge problem (Doyle and Teague 2006) lets students develop their own model and defend their choices with supporting mathematical arguments:

The Midge Problem

In 1981, two new varieties of a tiny biting insect called a midge were discovered by biologists Grogan and Wirth. They named one kind of midge an **Apf** midge and the other an **Af** midge. The biologists found out that the **Apf** midge is a carrier of a debilitating disease, while the other form of the midge, the **Af**, is quite harmless. In an effort to distinguish the two varieties, the biologist took measurements of wing length and antenna length on the midges they caught.

Af Midges
Wing length (cm): 1.72, 1.64, 1.74, 1.70, 1.82, 1.82, 1.90, 1.82, 2.08
Antenna length (cm): 1.24, 1.38, 1.36, 1.40, 1.38, 1.48, 1.38, 1.54, 1.56

Apf Midges
Wing length (cm): 1.78, 1.86, 1.96, 2.00, 2.00, 1.96
Antenna length (cm): 1.14, 1.20, 1.30, 1.26, 1.28, 1.18

Is it possible to distinguish an **Af** midge from an **Apf** midge on the basis of wing and antenna length? Write a report that describes to a naturalist in the field how to classify a midge that he or she has just captured.

Students are generally not accustomed to working on a problem that has no single, uncontested correct answer, and they are sometimes uncomfortable or uncertain of how to handle this situation. In the following exchange between a teacher and a group of students, the teacher helps the students focus on supporting their decision with clear, precise mathematical reasoning.

Student A: We created a scatterplot with antenna length on the *y*-axis and wing length on the *x*-axis.

Student B: We can tell that the points representing the **Af** and the **Apf** midges are in distinct regions, and we want to create a line that separates the two regions. The problem is that there are lots of ways to do that. How do we know which method is best?

Teacher: Great question! It depends on what you decide is most important. Let's consider a simple example. Notice that the largest antenna length on the **Apf** midges is 1.30 cm. Suppose my method for the naturalist is to classify all midges with antenna length greater than 1.30 cm as type **Af**. What do you think about this method? Be specific.

Student C: It would be very simple to use, which is good, but it doesn't seem like the best division of the two types.

Student A: I think it is a terrible method. You misclassified one of the **Af** midges. Plus, I think it is pretty likely that you could find an **Apf** midge with a slightly higher antenna length than 1.30 cm.

Student B: I agree. That would be a serious mistake, because we would miss one of the deadly midges.

Teacher: Notice that you analyzed the quality of my method on the basis of factors you believe are important. There are many possible methods. You need to create one that is based on clear, precise mathematics and satisfies the characteristics you think are important.

Students working on the problem in small groups have approached it in various ways. Approaches we have seen include the following (**Apf** midges are indicated with squares, and **Af** midges are indicated with circles):

1. Fit a line to both types, and find the midline between them, $y = 0.5185x + 0.350$. Any midge below this line is considered an **Apf** midge, whereas any midge above the line is considered an **Af** midge. Students should note that this method misclassifies one midge (but it is a "good" midge).

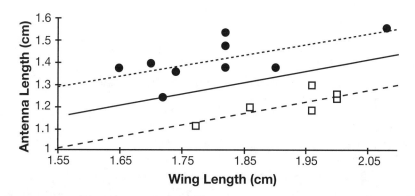

2. Find the equations of the lines defined by the two "outermost" midges in each group. As before, some students took the midline for the boundary, whereas others wanted to err on the side of caution and used the **Af** boundary line. Still others used a line weighted by the number of midges caught.

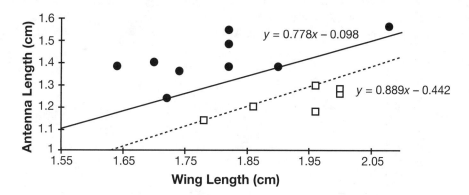

3. Students usually recognized that the **Af** midges have larger antennae and smaller wings, so the ratios of antenna to wing lengths might be useful. The smallest ratio for **Af** midges is 0.721 and the largest for **Apf** midges is 0.663. Groups differ on how to split up this interval [0.663, 0.721], some using the midpoint and others, recognizing that three-fifths of all the midges found have been **Af** midges, settled on a point three-fifths through the interval.

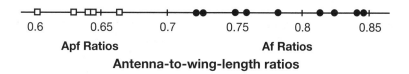

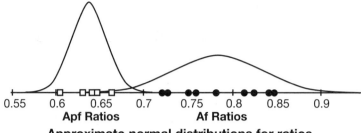

Apf Ratios   **Af Ratios**

Approximate normal distributions for ratios

From normal probability plots, students can argue that the **Af** ratios are approximately normally distributed, with a mean of 0.785 and standard deviation of 0.048, whereas the **Apf** ratios are approximately normally distributed, with a mean of 0.637 and a standard deviation of 0.020. Since the **Apf** ratios $\sim N(0.637, 0.020)$, students find that only 5 percent of **Apf** midges should have a ratio larger than 0.6699. Other groups look for the boundary that would determine where the midge is equally likely to be **Af** or **Apf**. A z score, computed as $z = \dfrac{x - \bar{x}}{s}$, measures the distance from the mean in standard deviations. Solving $\dfrac{x - 0.637}{0.020} = \dfrac{0.785 - x}{0.048}$, they find that $x = 0.6805$.

If the data are linear, the residuals from a least-squares fit should be approximately normally distributed. This means that close to 68 percent of the data will fall within one standard deviation of the residuals and 95 percent within 2 standard deviations. Using this information, they found a boundary at which the midge was equally likely to be **Af** or **Apf**.

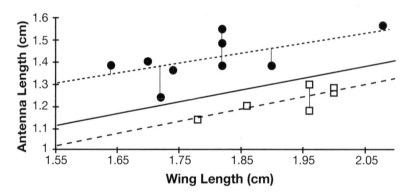

The midge problem challenges many students' preconceptions about mathematical problem solving. No single, correct solution exists, and students could use a wide range of skills, techniques, and approaches. Most important for developing the growth mindset: students must make their own decisions about how best to solve the problem and to defend their choices with mathematical reasoning. This experience can be powerful for students who previously thought of studying mathematics as simply learning procedures. By solving such problems, students recognize that they can create mathematics and gain confidence in their ability to face challenging problems.

Good Questions and Group-Worthy Problems

The Good Questions Project (Miller, Santana-Vega, and Terrell 2006) conducted in calculus classes at Cornell University illustrates the importance of student-to-student conversation on thought-provoking problems. This project used an active learning protocol in which the instructors paused periodically throughout the class to ask a highly conceptual multiple-choice or true–false question.

For example: "True or false: at one time, you were exactly π feet tall." The students are asked to vote by using a clicker system and then discuss among themselves why they believe their answer is correct; they also ask questions of those with different choices. Good questions have the following characteristics: (1) they force students to probe their understanding rather than their computational skill; (2) they reveal common misunderstandings while provoking student interest; (3) they promote student conjectures and require mathematical arguments to support their conjectures; and (4) at their heart, they are opportunities for reasoning and sense making, building a logical bridge from old to new knowledge, and making essential connections along the way. The research of Miller, Santana-Vega, and Terrell (2006) shows the overwhelmingly positive effects of consistently using good questions and the essential component of student-to-student conversation in their performance in calculus at Cornell.

Boaler (2002) described similarly the importance and effectiveness of what she terms "group-worthy problems." Group-worthy problems are open-ended problems that illustrate important mathematical concepts, allow for multiple representations and approaches, and have several solution paths that students could follow depending on what ideas the group has as they discuss the problem. Earlier, Boaler and Greeno (2000) found that students developed attitudes toward learning mathematics that were linked with the kinds of learning opportunities they had in class. They interviewed high school AP calculus students who were in classes that were either didactic, with individual work, or inquiry based, which encouraged collaboration and discussion. Their findings, as Gresalfi, Boaler, and Cobb (2004) described, showed that "many of the students who were enrolled in the didactic classes indicated that they felt that they had to give up agency and creativity if they were to take more advanced mathematics courses. In contrast, students who were enrolled in classes that were inquiry-based developed very different ideas about mathematics, and felt that it was a discipline with [*sic*] which gave them space to engage with mathematics in a creative way that went beyond memorization" (p. 2).

Appropriate Classroom and Curricular Experiences for Advanced Students

Although keeping control in the classroom is essential, we believe that allowing students to share different points of view, to teach and to learn from each other, is important also. Although the teacher is the authority on behavior in the classroom, students must see mathematics itself as the ultimate authority on what is correct or incorrect. As Skemp (1987) pointed out, "If a teacher makes a mistake when working on the blackboard and a member of the class points it out, the teacher has no alternative but to correct it. Teachers are subject to the same rules as learners, and these are not the rules of an authoritarian hierarchy, but of a shared structure of concepts. In mathematics perhaps more than any other subject the learning process depends on agreement, and this agreement rests on pure reason. . . . Learners have no need to accept anything which is not agreeable to their own intelligence— ideally they have a duty not to" (p. 85). Rules without reasons, to use Skemp's term, cannot produce understandable mathematics.

Following similar lines, Gresalfi, Boaler, and Cobb (2004, p. 6) note that "for students to develop an inquiring stance towards mathematics, they needed to believe that they had the authority to reason about ideas. It seems unlikely that students who saw mathematics as a set of rules that only the teacher or the textbook could validate would feel confident inquiring about mathematical problems."

Students need experiences that allow them to think like a mathematician, and so do their teachers. Students should be able to see their classmates struggle and share in their methods for getting unstuck. Equally important: students should be able to see their teachers struggle and share in their methods for getting unstuck. Having the teacher thinking aloud as they learn from an incorrect approach is an invaluable object lesson for students. Unfortunately, few high school teachers have had the kinds of true exploratory experiences described here, and the prospect of "not knowing" in front of one's students can be daunting, even frightening. Teachers must be comfortable living the experiences they want for their students and modeling the exploratory process as a part of their classroom activities. As teachers of mathematics, our task with all students—but especially with students who have strong interest in mathematics and obvious talent—is not just to teach mathematical content but also to teach students how to learn mathematics and to love the special challenge that mathematics uniquely offers. As teachers, we need to live that challenge as well.

Now few teachers have had these kinds of experiences either in their teacher preparation in college or in in-service or summer programs. Researchers for the Fordham Institute (Duffett, Farkas, and Loveless 2008) asked teachers how much their teacher preparation program emphasized teaching academically advanced students; only 5 percent indicated "a lot," whereas 30 percent listed "some," 46 percent said "very little," and 18 percent said "none at all." This is a particular need that could be met with the cooperation and support of the mathematical community and entities such as the Mathematical Association of America, the American Mathematical Society, the Society of Industrial and Applied Mathematics, the American Statistical Association, and industries in the mathematical sciences.

The goal of all teaching is to set a stage that enables students to take the information being presented and reconfigure it so that it makes sense in their own terms and so that the knowledge becomes personal and the students make the concepts their own. One way to accomplish this is through posing challenging questions for students and by challenging the answers they offer. Through this process, students gain a sense of power in and control over the mathematics under study, which allows them to tackle problems that are different from any encountered before.

In science, the goal is a hands-on curriculum that has students engaged in actual scientific inquiry. In mathematics, teachers create a "minds-on" mathematics curriculum by asking probing questions and giving support when and where needed while allowing students to develop many of the mathematical ideas themselves. A minds-on approach requires reasoning and sense making by giving students problems that they have not been explicitly taught how to solve but that reside in the knowledge in their zone of proximal development (Vygotsky 1978). In this way, students formulate a solution with their present knowledge, thereby extending their understanding of new situations.

However, this does not mean that teachers should expect students to do original mathematical research, although that is a possibility. It does mean that students should do mathematics that is new to them, that requires them to pull together familiar mathematical principles and extend them into new areas. Mathematical modeling offers many entry points into true mathematical investigations.

If students incur no difficulties in developing the solution, they do not need novel approaches to solve the problem. The truly creative approach comes often from students whose first (or second) approach leads to a dead end. Deciding how to circumvent this dead end often leads to creative insight. An example in which this attribute is needed is the Michael Jordan problem (North Carolina School of Science and Mathematics 1999).

Such problems can become mini research projects, small at first, but more and more sophisticated as the students move through their coursework and develop their knowledge base and modeling expertise. In *Making Calculus Students Think with Research Projects*, Cohen and colleagues (1994, p. 194) described the guiding principle: "The idea of student research projects is to pose problems much harder than typical homework problems and give students one or two weeks to do them. . . . The object is to give the students an idea of mathematical research, to have them learn the agony and ecstasy of intellectual discovery. We want to give students a taste of doing mathematics as mathematicians do it. After 12 years of study, shouldn't students have some idea of what professionals in the field do?"

In mathematical modeling or any complex mathematical task, progress often comes from repeated partial failures. Learning to expect and use errors fruitfully is essential to progress. This is a difficult challenge for students who are used to 95 percent proficiency every two weeks. Students who experience modeling as an integral component of their curriculum come to value different approaches and value learning from false starts.

The Michael Jordan Problem

A basketball player was driving to the basket and was fouled. As he stood at the free-throw line, the announcer stated that so far this year, the player had made 78% of his free throws. On this occasion, he made one and missed one. Later in the game, the player was again fouled. As he stood at the free-throw line, the announcer gave his updated stats; he had now made 76% of his free throws. How many free throws had the player made at that point in the season?

Most students' initial response is to set up and solve a system of equations. If a represents the number of attempts and s represents the number of successes, then $s/a = 0.78$ and $(s + 1)/(a + 2) = 0.76$. This system of equations is a standard problem in secondary algebra. Unfortunately, this formulation requires the player to have made 20.28 shots of 26 attempts. Clearly this "solution" is lacking. Where do the students go from here?

Upon reflection, students realize the percentages have been rounded. We really have a system of inequalities: $0.775 \le (s/a) < 0.785$ and $0.755 \le (s + 1)/(a + 2) < 0.765$. These inequalities define a long, thin quadrilateral in the plane as. Students must devise a method of searching the interior of a quadrilateral for lattice points, a process that none of the students have been taught. The variety of approaches students use may be found in the Michael Jordan problem (Goebel and Teague 1998). Once they have devised a method for searching the region for lattice points, students find that the system of inequalities actually has six different solutions:

s	18	21	25	28	31	38
a	23	27	32	36	40	49
$\dfrac{s}{a} \approx 0.78$	0.7826	0.7778	0.7813	0.7778	0.7750	0.7755
$\dfrac{s+1}{a+2} \approx 0.76$	0.7600	0.7586	0.7647	0.7632	0.7619	0.7647

Challenges such as the Michael Jordan problem require creativity from the students since they have no known algorithm to fall back on.

* * *

In the Driving for Gas problem (see next page), students need to decide which of the many possible variables are important to include in the model and what is too complicated to include. They consider the car's mileage per gallon, the size of the gas tank, and the distance to the gas station. They consider various driving habits, value of time lost, and many other factors in their model, but they typically decide that they must leave these out if they are to have any hope of creating a model that contains the essence of the problem and is still tractable with the mathematical tools they know.

David Bressoud (2006), MAA president, comments, "Students learn how to apply mathematical insights to problems outside of mathematics by practicing doing it. This is what modeling is all about. Modeling is seldom done well, especially when attempted in the context of a course with a prescribed set of skills and concepts that must be mastered. Real modeling is messy and time consuming. If we want students to learn how to transfer these skills and concepts, we cannot teach the mathematical topic and then seek applications. We must start by giving students a problem that does not quite fit into any of the categories they know how to handle" (p. 1).

Driving for Gas

Every driver recognizes the weekly fluctuations in gas prices. In some areas, a local radio station has a special report on the location of the gas station with the lowest price per gallon. Is it worth the drive across town for cheaper gas? If you know the locations and the prices at two stations, at which one should you buy your gas? Does it depend on the car you are driving, and if so, how?

Does it matter if you think that you are buying gallons of gas or buying miles of travel? Develop a model that owners of different cars can use that will tell them how far they should be willing to drive according to the specifications of their car.

Even simple problems can enable student creativity and ownership of the mathematics. Consider the cookie problem (Compton and Teague 1996):

The Cookie Problem

The bakery currently sells 1000 large chocolate chip cookies each week for $0.50 each. A survey convinced the manager that for every $0.10 increase, the bakery would sell 70 fewer cookies each week. At what price should the cookies be sold to maximize the revenue to the bakery?

If the teacher encourages student thought but doesn't prescribe a specific approach, then any number of interesting approaches will appear. The following includes examples of student models:

The revenue, R, is the product of the price charged, p, and the number of cookies sold, C. So, $R = p \times C$. For each 10-cent increase in price, the demand is reduced by 70 cookies. The slope of the line is $m = -7 \dfrac{\text{cookies}}{\text{cent increase}}$. Since the bakery presently sells 1000 cookies at 50 cents each, the point (50, 1000) lies on the line. So $C = -7(p - 50) + 1000 = -7p + 1350$. The revenue, then, is given by $R(p) = p(-7p + 1350)$. This is a quadratic function, and the p-coordinate of the vertex of this parabola represents the optimum price.

The students then find the vertex in one of several ways:

- Recall from algebra the location of the vertex of the quadratic $y = ax^2 + bx + c$ is $x = \dfrac{-b}{2a}$, or here, $p = \dfrac{-1350}{-14} = 96.43$.

- The zeros are $p = 0$ and $p = \dfrac{1350}{7}$, so the vertex is $p = \dfrac{(\frac{1350}{7} + 0)}{2} = 96.43$ in this problem.

- Graph the revenue function $R(p) = p(-7p + 1350)$ on their calculators and seek the price that yields the numerical maximum for revenue, which is reported as $p = 96.43$.

Or, students first developed a table of price and demand:

Price	50	60	70	80	90	100	110	120
Demand	1000	930	860	790	720	650	580	510

They then used their calculators to fit the regression line relating price to demand. This line is $y = -7x + 1350$ and created the revenue function $R = xy = x(-7x + 1350)$.

Others multiplied the two rows in the table together and created a table with revenue:

Price	50	60	70	80	90	100	110	120
Demand	1,000	930	860	790	720	650	580	510
Revenue	50,000	55,800	60,200	63,200	64,800	65,000	63,800	61,200

Some students simply looked on the chart and reported the optimum price as $1.00 and the expected revenue as $650.00 or used the calculator to fit a quadratic function to the data (price, revenue) by using quadratic regression and found the vertex.

Students could use dime increases, d, from 50 cents as the independent variable, so $p = (0.50 + 0.1d)$, with demand $D = (1000 - 70d)$, so $R(d) = (0.50 + 0.1d)(1000 - 70d)$. The vertex of this parabola is at $d = 65/14 = 4.64$—so students can expect that there should be an increase of 46 cents from 50 cents.

Students could set the independent variable as the number of cookies sold. The number of cookies lost, L, is 700 times the increase in price measured in dollars, I, so $I = \dfrac{L}{700}$ here. The price we charge is $0.50 + I$. If C is the number of cookies sold, then the number of cookie sales lost due to increasing the price is $L = 1000 - C$, and the price we charge is $\left(0.5 + \dfrac{1000 - C}{700}\right)$. So,

$R(C) = C\left(0.5 + \dfrac{1000 - C}{700}\right)$. This is also a quadratic function with a vertex at $C = 675$. This means the

best price to charge is $\left(0.5 + \dfrac{1000 - 675}{700}\right) = 0.96$.

For an exercise, work out the student's thought processes in developing this correct model,

$R(x) = x\left(1000 - \left(\dfrac{x - 0.5}{0.1}\right)70\right).$

Those students moving into areas of applied mathematics and engineering obviously benefit from their modeling experiences. But those entering programs in pure mathematics benefit as well, though in different ways. The creative aspects of modeling can open the students' eyes to the joy of mathematical discovery as well as the development of that elusive mathematical maturity. Engaging modeling activities free them from the tyranny of technique that has dominated most of their mathematical experiences. Students are using mathematics to make sense of the world around them and consequently come to expect mathematics to make sense—and further, they expect to understand it. This expectation is an important but seldom-mentioned aspect of understanding the importance of proof.

Proof and Mathematical Rigor for Advanced Students

Perhaps the first requirement of proof in mathematics is an expectation on the student's part that the mathematics should make sense and be supportable by reasoned argument. If students do not expect mathematics to be sensible, proof can have little value to the student and becomes just one more thing to memorize. University of Chicago mathematician Saunders MacLane (1994) has suggested that the sequence of mathematical understanding is

intuition → trial → error → speculation → conjecture → proof

For secondary students beginning their serious study of mathematics, we would expand MacLane's sequence a bit:

exploration → intuition → trial → error → insight → conjecture → reasoned argument → proof

This sequence of events describes mathematical investigation and mathematical discovery. The entire process of mathematical discovery is mathematical rigor writ large: doing authentic, creative mathematics. This process of creating a model, making strong assumptions and conditions, solving a simple case and generalizing the results, modifying the conditions to strengthen the results, and presenting your work in a way that convinces the [reader, audience, . . .] that you have it right captures the essence of the mathematical spirit, and it can begin early in the students' schooling if modeling and sense making are at the core of the curriculum.

Create a Learning Environment that Supports Student Creativity for All Students

The first responsibility of the teacher is to ensure that the learning environment supports student creativity and investigation. The learning environment must be one that supports students and teachers in taking risks and one that sees failures as fresh opportunities from which to learn and grow. Parents, the community, the school administration, teachers, and students all have a role to play in creating such an environment. If the parents or community requires using only objective test scores to measure learning, creativity can be stifled before it has a chance to flourish. If administrators expect students to sit quietly in rows, progressing all at the same rate, then neither teachers nor students are likely to value creativity highly.

All students can engage in creative problem solving and will profit from adding something of themselves to their explorations. Giving them an environment that supports, encourages, and motivates them to do so is essential. If students' creative solutions are respected and encouraged early in their mathematical studies, then the students will develop stronger interests in mathematics.

Encouraging all students to generalize and extend the problems discussed in class is one way of creating a supportive learning environment. Seeing structure in the problems is essential, as is developing understanding of how mathematics depends on that structure. The focus should not be on demonstrating how to do the problems; rather, an emphasis on sharing ideas and communicating thinking will help students grow in their understanding of the mathematical ideas they study. How groups are determined should vary. At times, grouping the students by ability level is preferable so that the most advanced students can work together on higher-level problems and share their ideas and approaches with each other. At other times, forming groups of students with varied ability levels can help advanced students develop their own thinking and can be helpful to other students.

In a heterogeneous classroom, levels of talent, interest, and ability vary among the students. A classroom in which a few students stand out in their ability and interest in mathematics proves to be a challenge for teachers, who can find ensuring that they are serving every student difficult. Teachers must challenge these advanced students without simply giving them more and harder work. Students might consider themselves punished, as opposed to encouraged and supported, for their success and interest in mathematics. We want students to feel that they have opportunities, not chores.

Several ways exist to challenge advanced students in a heterogeneous classroom. One is to include carefully chosen open-ended problems in their assignments. Give students the option of doing, for example, six of nine problems, allowing everyone access to questions at a variety of levels of challenge. If a standard graded assignment has six ten-point problems, include two more extensive twenty-five-point problems and one forty-point problem that requires significant creativity and effort.

Then have each student turn in problems worth at least sixty points. This way, students can select problems that most interest them, and the students choosing the more demanding problems aren't being punished by having to do all the "regular" problems and then some additional ones. Equally important: all students have the opportunity to tackle a more challenging problem if they choose. As the class progresses, more students will choose one challenge problem rather than two or three of the more standard fare.

Another way to challenge advanced students is to offer bonus questions worth few points relative to the total points possible, thereby offering a small reward for the students' efforts. In this way, the less advanced students will not be harmed if they cannot find a solution, whereas the more advanced students will be challenged to find one.

A third method of challenging students is to devote a bulletin board in the classroom to ongoing challenge problems and to offer students a few bonus points for turning in a thorough and thoughtful solution. The students could even be required to present their solutions to the rest of the class, thereby giving them another challenge: communicating their understanding to others more formally.

Teachers can also encourage their students to participate in mathematics contests by announcing and advertising such events in class. They can also encourage students to form or participate in math clubs on campus, in their communities, or even online. This way, students can share their interests with other students who are not necessarily in their class or studying the same material.

Mathematical Challenges for All

The curriculum and classroom experiences designed for advanced students are rooted in student engagement, in problems that pull the students forward in their understanding of mathematics as they grapple with the mathematical challenges. Such a curriculum requires teachers who are just as interested and willing to stretch themselves as they expect their students to be. And although the topics and particular problems posed will differ from those in other classes, the fundamental features of students actively engaged in mathematical thinking and sense making are the same for all mathematics classrooms. What we want for students of mathematical talent and interest is what we want for all students. The basic principles of good teaching are essential for all students at all levels of their mathematics education.

References

American Mathematical Society (AMS). "Reports of the AMS Association Resource Group." *Notices of the AMS* 45, no. 2 (1997): 276.

Bennett, Jennie, Manuel Berriozabal, Margaret DeArmond, Linda Sheffield, and Richard Wertheimer. "Report of the NCTM Task Force on the Mathematically Promising." In *Developing Mathematically Promising Students*, edited by Linda Sheffield, pp. 309–16. Reston, Va.: National Council of Teachers of Mathematics, 1999.

Bleske-Rechek, April, David Lubinski, and Camilla P. Benbow. "Meeting the Educational Needs of Special Populations." *Psychological Science* 15 (April 2004): 217–24.

Boaler, Jo. *Experiencing School Mathematics.* 2nd ed. London: Routledge, 2002.

Boaler, Jo, and J. G. Greeno. "Identity, Agency, and Knowing in Mathematical Worlds." In *Multiple Perspectives on Mathematics Teaching and Learning*, edited by Jo Boaler, pp. 171–200. Westport, Conn.: Ablex Publishing, 2000.

Bressoud, David M. "Launchings from the CUPM Curriculum Guide: Teaching for Transference." Mathematical Association of America. January 2006. www.maa.org/columns/launchings/launchings_01_06.html.

Cohen, Marcus, Arthur Knoebel, Douglas S. Kurtz, and David J. Pengelley. *Making Calculus Students Think with Research Projects*, edited by Alan H. Schoenfeld. New Jersey Hove, UK: Lawrence Erlbaum, 1994.

Colangelo, Nicholas, Susan G. Assouline, and Miraca U. M. Gross. *A Nation Deceived: How Schools Hold Back Our Brightest Students.* Templeton National Report on Acceleration. Iowa City, Iowa: Connie Belin and Jacqueline N. Blank International Center for Gifted Education and Talent Development, 2004.

Compton, Helen, and Dan Teague. "The Cookie Problem." *Consortium* (COMAP Inc.), no. 59 (Fall 1996): Everybody's Problems.

Doyle, Dot, and Dan Teague. "The Midge Problem Revisited." *Consortium* (COMAP Inc.), no. 91 (Fall/Winter 2006): Everybody's Problems.

Duffett, Ann, Steve Farkas, and Tom Loveless. *High-Achieving Students in the Era of NCLB.* Fordham Study. Washington, D.C.: Thomas B. Fordham Institute, 2008.

Dweck, Carol. *Mindset: The New Psychology of Success.* New York: Random House, 2006.

Goebel, John, and Dan Teague. "The Michael Jordan Problem." *Consortium* (COMAP Inc.), no. 68 (Winter 1998): Everybody's Problems.

Goodkin, Susan. "Leave No Gifted Child Behind." *Washington Post.* December 27, 2005. www.washingtonpost.com/wp-dyn/content/article/2005/12/26/AR2005122600553.html (accessed August 25, 2010).

Gresalfi, Melissa, Nick Fiori, Jo Boaler, and Paul Cobb. "Exploring an Elusive Link between Knowledge and Practice." North American Chapter of the International Group for the Psychology of Mathematics Education. 2004. www.allacademic.com//meta/p_mla_apa_research_citation/1/1/7/5/0/pages117506/p117506-2.php (accessed August 25, 2010).

Kennedy, Dan. "Assessing True Academic Success: The Next Frontier of Reform." *Mathematics Teacher* 92 (September 1999): 462.

———. "Is the AP Program Still Good for Mathematics Education?" Paper presented at the 83rd annual meeting of the National Council of Teachers of Mathematics, Anaheim, Calif., April 2005.

Krakovsky, Marina. "The Effort Effect." *Stanford Magazine.* March–April 2007. www.stanfordalumni.org/news/magazine/2007/marapr/features/dweck.html (accessed August 25, 2010).

MacLane, Saunders. "Responses to 'Theoretical Mathematics: Toward A Cultural Synthesis of Mathematics and Theoretical Physics' by A. Jaffe and F. Quinn." *Bulletin of the American Mathematical Society* 30 (April 1994): 191.

Mathematical Association of America (MAA). "Second Report from the Task Force." June 17, 1997. www.maa.org/past/maanctm3.html (accessed August 25, 2010).

Miller, Robyn L., Everilis Santana-Vega, and Maria S. Terrell. "Can Good Questions and Peer Discussion Improve Calculus Instruction?" *PRIMUS* 16 (September 2006): 193–203.

National Association for Gifted Children (NAGC). "State of the Nation in Gifted Education: How States Regulate and Support Programs and Services for Gifted and Talented Students—An Executive Summary of the *State of the States* Report." 2009. www.nagc.org/uploadedFiles/Information_and_Resources/State_of_the_States_2008-2009/2008-09%20State%20of%20the%20Nation%20overview.pdf.

National Council of Teachers of Mathematics (NCTM). "An Agenda for Action: Recommendations for School Mathematics of the 1980s." 1980. www.nctm.org/standards/content.aspx?id=17278 (accessed August 25, 2010).

———. *Principles and Standards for School Mathematics.* Reston, Va.: NCTM, 2000.

National Research Council. *Learning and Understanding: Improving Advanced Study of Mathematics and Science.* Mathematics Panel Report. Washington, D.C.: National Academies Press, 2002.

North Carolina School of Science and Mathematics. *Contemporary Precalculus through Applications.* 2nd ed. Chicago: Everyday Learning Corp., 1999.

Renzulli, Joseph. "The Three-Ring Conception of Giftedness: A Developmental Model for Creative Productivity." Paper presented at the 68th annual meeting of the American Educational Research Association, New Orleans, 1984.

Saul, Mark. "A Community of Scholars: Working with Students of High Ability in the High School." In *Developing Mathematically Promising Students*, edited by Linda Jensen Sheffield, pp. 81–92. Reston, Va.: National Council of Teachers of Mathematics, 1999.

Schoenfeld, Alan H. "When Good Teaching Leads to Bad Results: The Disasters of 'Well-Taught' Mathematics Courses." *Educational Psychologist* 23 (March 1988): 145–66.

———. "The Math Wars." *Educational Policy* 18 (January–March 2004): 253–86.

Skemp, Richard R. *The Psychology of Learning Mathematics: Expanded American Edition.* 2nd ed. Hillsdale, N.J.: Lawrence Erlbaum, 1987.

Stanley, Julian C., and Camilla Persson Benbow. "Educating Mathematically Precocious Youths: Twelve Policy Recommendations." *Educational Researcher* 11 (May 1982): 4–9.

Tobias, Sheila. *They're Not Dumb, They're Different: Stalking the Second Tier.* Tucson, Ariz.: Research Corp., 1990.

Vygotsky, Lev S. *Mind in Society: Development of Higher Psychological Processes.* Cambridge, Mass.: Harvard University Press, 1978.

Chapter 5

Mathematical Reasoning and Sense Making Begins with the Opportunity to Learn

Lee V. Stiff and Janet L. Johnson

Principles and Standards for School Mathematics (National Council of Teachers of Mathematics [NCTM] 2000) is a blueprint for high-quality mathematics for every child. These Standards can help curriculum developers build curricula that are coherent across the grades, focused on both mathematical content and process, and supportive of excellence in teaching and learning mathematics. Standards-based programs can help students learn mathematics with understanding, acquire basic skills and in-depth knowledge of more and better mathematics, and develop reasoning and sense-making skills to become resourceful and flexible problem solvers. However, none of the benefits of *Principles and Standards* matters if students are denied access to the curricula and instruction created to achieve the vision of the Standards. Moreover, if assessments are not aligned with Standards-based curricula and instruction, then a coherent and cohesive mathematics program that promotes mathematical reasoning and sense making will probably not be achieved (NCTM 2009).

The problem of student access to high-quality curricula and instruction is a subset of the many equity concerns that plague horribly equipped schools staffed by underqualified, or even unqualified, teachers of mathematics. As recounted by Kozol (1991), long before issues related to the benefits of Standards-based programs are explored, far too many poor and minority children face shortages of textbooks and supplies, learning tools, and quality classroom environments. Even poor and minority students attending affluent schools find themselves segregated into "low-performing classes" taught by underprepared teachers (Stiff, Johnson, and Akos, forthcoming).

A variety of issues that go beyond the mathematics classroom undoubtedly affect the opportunity to learn mathematics. It may be these issues that convince many educators that poor and minority students are doomed to underachievement in school and in mathematics in particular. Knowing that students are at risk ought to inspire teachers to create strategies that prevent failure in schools. Too often, however, this knowledge gives educators an excuse to stop giving all students access to quality curricula and instruction and the best opportunities to learn.

If all students should have access to mathematics curricula that promote reasoning and sense making, then all students should be properly evaluated to determine the types of experiences they need to maximize their mathematical learning. In particular, curriculum choices and course-taking opportunities afforded students should be based on objective feedback tied to student performance. Unfortunately, this is often not the case; curriculum choices and course-taking opportunities are typically linked to student demographics.

Opportunity to Learn and the At-Risk Model

The nature of students' opportunity to learn mathematics usually depends on whether the adults in students' lives—school personnel—view them as being at risk. At-risk models for helping students revolve around decisions based on perceived student demographics and characteristics such as ethnicity, gender, family income level, learning style, learning disability, and past achievement (Schwartz 1988). If students are deemed as being at risk, then schools offer them services pursuant to that classification. In mathematics, a common outcome of being designated at risk is that students receive remedial instruction. Remedial instruction often takes place in the "low" or "regular" tracks in middle school and high school. After students are placed into these lower tracks of the curriculum, their opportunity to learn high-quality mathematics, including mathematical reasoning and sense making, is adversely affected (Burris and Welnar 2005; Callahan 2005). In fact, most students placed in the lower tracks find themselves in a downward trajectory in mathematics that can detrimentally affect their future in mathematics and ultimately their lives. After students have been tracked low, they usually remain in the low track, and the achievement gaps between students tracked high and students tracked low become greater over time (Wheelock 1992; O'Connor, Lewis, and Mueller 2007). Furthermore, the evidence suggests that assigning students to the lower tracks depresses learning regardless of their ability levels (Hallinan 2003).

In contrast, affording students opportunities to take more worthwhile mathematics helps them perform better. For example, Burris, Heubert, and Levin (2006) analyzed how tracking affected students with similar math abilities. Students placed in the top mathematics track had greater success in their future schooling. After high average (C+) middle school students were placed in low, regular, and advanced mathematics courses, 2 percent of those in the low track, 23 percent of those in the regular track, and 91 percent of those in the high track successfully completed two college-prep mathematics courses in high school.

At-risk models create obstacles to offering students the learning opportunities that they otherwise deserve. Beliefs and attitudes about at-risk students often override other indications about their capacity to perform in courses that engage their mathematical reasoning and sense-making skills. Non-Asian minorities who are as qualified as their Asian and white counterparts are less likely to be placed in the more rigorous mathematics courses (Vanfossen, Jones, and Spade 1987; O'Connor, Lewis, and Mueller 2007). In fact, many students who *can* achieve simply never get the opportunity. In one school district, for example, of the students who demonstrated the ability to be placed into algebra, only 51 percent of black students and 42 percent of Latino students were admitted, whereas all Asian students and 88 percent of white students were (Stone and Turba 1999).

The real danger of using at-risk models to serve student needs is how doing so affects students' mathematical self-efficacy. Here, we view mathematical self-efficacy as students' beliefs about their capacity to perform in the mathematics classroom and exercise control over events that affect that performance. In general, self-efficacy beliefs affect how people feel, think, and behave; self-efficacy belief also affects their motivation to achieve. Students' beliefs about their efficacy are developed largely through four main sources of influences: (1) life experiences, (2) social modeling, (3) social persuasion, and (4) emotional and somatic states (Bandura 1994). In the context of teaching and learning mathematics, each source of influence plays an important role in students' success and affects their opportunity to learn.

Engaging mathematics content successfully creates life experiences that strengthen students' sense of mathematical self-efficacy. Failure to understand mathematics content—or worse, not having the opportunity to engage worthwhile mathematics content—undermines and weakens mathematical self-efficacy. Positive and rewarding classroom experiences in mathematics create a foundation on which future success can be built. Research cites the positive academic benefits of treating all students as high achievers (Hallinan 2000; Garrity 2004; Burris, Heubert, and Levin 2006) and reinforces the need teachers should feel to create more opportunities for students to engage in mathematical reasoning and sense making. In mathematics classrooms, life experiences should reflect the sentiment that is widely attributed to writer–philosopher Ayn Rand: "The ladder of success is best climbed by stepping on the rungs of opportunity."

Another influence on mathematical self-efficacy is social modeling, or observing how others perform in mathematics classrooms. If those being observed are socially similar to the observer, then the influence on the observer's self-efficacy is positive if those being observed are succeeding. If, however, none or few of the students who perform well are socially similar to the student observer, then the influence on the observer's self-efficacy is negative. Even if students themselves recognize that they should be in high-performing mathematics classrooms, many choose "places of respect" instead. That is, students choose mathematics courses and class settings in which they are not racially and socially isolated and that value their cultural backgrounds and dispositions (Yonezawa, Wells, and Serna 2002). If the number of minority and low-income students in high-track mathematics classes is small or nonexistent, these groups of students may develop poor mathematical self-efficacy no matter how strong their individual abilities may be. Because at-risk models view members of the group as alike, far too many high-performing minority and low-income students are treated as if they were low performing and are therefore deprived of the opportunity to study mathematics with their high-achieving peers (Mayer 2008; Abu El-Haj and Rubin 2009).

A third source of influence that affects students' opportunity to learn is social persuasion. One can argue that positive social persuasion is an essential activity that mathematics teachers should perform daily in class. In particular, teachers should convince students that they have the requisite skills and abilities to succeed in mathematics. Social persuasion in the mathematics classroom incorporates teaching strategies, approaches, and tools that promote student–teacher behaviors that lead to student success.

Stiff and Harvey (1988) described these behaviors in the context of identity, validity, and security. Social persuasion uses students' existing knowledge, skills, and understandings as a foundation for building new understandings. By incorporating what they have learned, students can be convinced that they already know what is needed to succeed; they come to believe that they deserve access to high-quality mathematics. This access creates a sense of belonging, of identity. Social persuasion also validates students. That is, when teachers hold high expectations and make students responsible for their own learning by requiring active participation in mathematically rigorous lessons, students get the message that teachers believe in their abilities. Validation of their abilities empowers students. And finally, social persuasion establishes and reinforces teachers' accountability to students. The use of social persuasion shows students that teachers do care and will do their part to foster meaningful opportunities for success in mathematics. Such assurances give students a sense of security and make facing new mathematical challenges easier for them.

At-risk models do not promote learning outcomes associated with positive social persuasion because at-risk models accept low expectations for students and in so doing actually discourage students from applying their abilities to succeed (Jamar and Pitts 2005; Akey 2006). This lack of support creates emotional dissonance for high-performing students.

Students' emotional disposition to engage mathematics content, and stress levels pursuant to any situation in which students might lose face, can affect how students feel about their ability to perform in mathematics classes. This final source of influence on mathematical self-efficacy is real and affects many students who find themselves in a position of having to "prove themselves" to teachers or other students. Students' perceptions of their mathematical abilities are important to how they engage in mathematical reasoning and sense making. An absence of feelings of accomplishment is directly linked to students' desire to engage in challenging mathematics (Pintrich and Schunk 1996; Akey 2006).

At-risk models for serving the needs of students often negatively affect these four sources of self-efficacy. Otherwise-capable students who are placed into lower mathematics tracks show decreased mathematical self-efficacy (Akos, Shoffner, and Ellis 2007; Callahan 2005). This finding is expected because at-risk students who have performed well in the past are consistently placed in lower mathematics tracks, thus creating real-life experiences in which performances that should be acknowledged and rewarded with greater opportunities to excel are not (Johnson et al. 2005).

Over time, at-risk students who have performed well come to believe that they are not good enough to succeed in mathematics because of their mathematics placement. That at-risk models treat students of the same demographic group in the same way exacerbates this situation. For example, if low-income students are assumed to be underachieving, then almost all low-income students will be placed into lower tracks. Placing low-income students into the lower tracks eliminates role models (social modeling) who would otherwise demonstrate that low-income students can excel in mathematics learning.

Because at-risk models are used to assign students to lower mathematics tracks, teacher exhortations (positive social persuasion) that students are capable of learning high-quality mathematics and engaging in mathematical reasoning and sense making ring hollow. Combined with inappropriate instruction and teacher beliefs about social barriers and lack of support (negative social persuasion), students face the prospects of lowered expectations and the resulting lower grades that ultimately affect their long-term college and career choices. And this scenario disproportionately affects minorities (Akos, Shoffner, and Ellis 2007).

The deleterious effects of low self-efficacy can cause anxiety (an emotional and somatic state), which neurologically affects cognition and performance (Gray, Braver, and Raichle 2002). So, when capable students are placed into low-track mathematics classes, their performance becomes worse, their confidence is weakened, and their opportunity to engage in mathematical reasoning and sense making is dramatically reduced.

In one statewide study, researchers observed just how prevalent at-risk models were. Educators revealed how they used demographic factors instead of objective academic criteria to make student placement and instructional intervention decisions. Specifically, the researchers asked school counselors whether they used academic data to determine how students should be placed into mathematics courses or which academic interventions to recommend. The counselors reported that they used both academic and behavioral data to decide about student services. However, when asked to describe the data that they used, many described free or reduced-price lunch status as academic data. A few school counselors even reported that because they lacked demographic data about students' socioeconomic status, they had to rely on race to indicate which students had barriers to learning and therefore would benefit from counseling services or referrals for academic interventions (Johnson et al. 2005).

For placement in mathematics courses, students' race and ethnicity or economic status as viewed through the lenses of at-risk models can apparently trump academic and performance data. Moreover, using a combination of demographic factors makes it possible for educators to knowingly or unknowingly track students by race and ethnicity. Mathematics course placement decisions based on demographic information negatively affect—and possibly create—the achievement gap and diminish future learning opportunities (Stiff, Johnson, and Akos, forthcoming).

In the most fundamental way, students who are placed into the lower tracks in mathematics have less access to high-quality instruction because more out-of-field mathematics teachers are assigned to teach them (Tate and Rousseau 2002; Peske and Haycock 2006). Combine this reality with the general observation that students taught by appropriately qualified mathematics teachers outperform students taught by less qualified mathematics teachers (Goldhaber and Brewer 2000; Darling-Hammond, Berry, and Thoreson 2001; Laczko-Kerr and Berliner 2002; Lubienski and Crockett 2007), and you see that at-risk students are not likely to receive opportunities for reasoning and sense making in mathematics classrooms. This supposition is especially true when one considers that underqualified mathematics teachers are more likely to work in high-minority, low-income schools (Education Trust 2008).

Using at-risk models is at the heart of lost opportunities in school mathematics. And if "well-meaning teachers and administrators cause inequity through practices that create biases they do not intend" (NCTM 2009, p. 93), such practices must be eliminated. Although middle schools and high schools that use at-risk models for placing students into mathematics courses are encouraged to offer opportunities for mathematical reasoning and sense making in every track, and to move students from lower tracks to higher ones, the evidence suggests that such schools seldom implement such remedies (Mallery and Mallery 1999; Stiff, Johnson, and Akos, forthcoming). In fact, the way to give students better opportunities to reason and make sense of mathematics is to eliminate lower tracks in school mathematics. Doing so should be the goal of school mathematics. An intermediate step toward this goal is the use of student performance/achievement data to make placement decisions instead of the demographic data that at-risk models use.

Opportunity to Learn and the Pro-Equity Model

A pro-equity model uses data to identify the types of support and instructional interventions that students need. It uses objective data about student performance and achievement to make decisions about the type of future opportunities that students should be offered. Pro-equity models use formative assessments to monitor and reassess ongoing student needs; they evaluate student needs on the basis of previous performance and achievement. Pro-equity models do not use perceived student demographics and characteristics such as ethnicity, gender, family income level, learning style, learning disability, and unsubstantiated past achievement to determine the services that students require. As noted, many educators believe that they are using a pro-equity model when they are really using an at-risk model for helping students. In such cases, educators cannot distinguish demographic data from objective performance data. This approach can create situations in which well-meaning teachers and administrators establish inequitable practices that eliminate opportunities for students to engage in mathematical reasoning and sense making in high-quality mathematics courses (Stiff, Johnson, and Akos, forthcoming).

A significant reason for the misunderstanding about objective performance data is the vocabulary that educators use to describe students. In professional development situations, when mathematics teachers, counselors, and administrators report that they have implemented instructional interventions or placed students into lower tracks in mathematics because students were low achieving, the data show that these students are generally low-income and minority students, many of whom are high achieving. Most school districts define *at-risk students* to mean students belonging to a given demographic group, such as low-income or black. These districts routinely place their at-risk students into intervention programs and/or remedial instruction in mathematics, whereas districts often ignore students who need instructional interventions but have no at-risk factors.

We created and field-tested simple icons designed and named to help educators change their thinking about so-called at-risk students. These icons help educators better communicate important ideas about helping students by using a vocabulary that forms the basis for rethinking their attitudes and beliefs about children and by establishing new paradigms about the achievement of low-income and minority students. We intend to demonstrate how using objective performance data to identify needed student services is superior to using demographic data as risk factors. This approach of developing powerful graphics for communicating quantitative information (Tufte 2001) has fostered avenues of communication that did not exist among educators.

Figure 5.1 presents terminology and icons to establish new conditions for reexamining information about students and schools. A prism illustrates that student data may be separated into different types of information. Some student information indicates no need for services, whereas other student information does. Student information that suggests a need for improving or correcting a situation is referred to as a "service indicator." Service indicators exist for both student data and school data.

Representing student data A prism helps educators see that different kinds of student data exist, as do different purposes for using those data.	
Demographic characteristics: Student/family data Ethnicity and race Income Gender	 Oranges
Service indicators: Student data EOG and EOC scores Attendance records Suspension records Formative and summative assessments	 Apples
Service indicators: School-based data Student classifications (e.g., BEH, AG, ADHD) School suspension patterns Enrollment data by ethnicity, race, and income Schoolwide attendance records Academic growth of students Teacher quality	 Mangos
Intangible factors: Student/family/school-based data Parental support Resources in the home Student potential and motivation Family life Academic dispositions of the schools Financial resources of the schools	 Worms

Fig. 5.1. Constructs and terminology associated with pro-equity models (EOG, end of grade; EOC, end of course; BEH, behaviorally or emotionally handicapped; AG, academically gifted; ADHD, attention deficit–hyperactivity disorder)

The metaphor of fruit describes the data (fig. 5.1). Oranges represent student attributes or characteristics that cannot be changed (generally, demographic characteristics such as race or ethnicity, family income, and gender). Apples represent student attributes or characteristics that we can assess and exert some influence over. These controllable factors include student performance on end-of-grade (EOG) or end-of-course (EOC) assessments, longitudinal data on student achievement, student behavior in school, and school attendance. Mangos represent school-based data—subjective factors that affect the services and opportunities to which students have access. We describe these as subjective factors because assumptions that teachers and administrators make about students or the services they require typically influence the data. The mango category includes the following: student classifications (e.g., behaviorally/emotionally handicapped, academically gifted, and attention deficit–hyperactivity disorder), policy consequences (e.g., school suspension practices or scheduling classes in such a way that prevents certain students from having access to high-track mathematics courses), quality of instruction, and school placement practices.

To extend the metaphor: each type of fruit may have worms. The concept of worms represents intangible factors. This is information that a data set cannot easily measure, such as parental support, student motivation, and resources in the home, or information that reflects attitudes and cultural beliefs about groups of students, such as the number of mathematics course offerings in the low tracks and the allocation of financial resources to remedial programs versus that to high-track course offerings. Worms often become the way that educators describe groups of students to justify decisions about the services they receive.

New terminology makes it possible to ponder whether at-risk students ought to be considered for opportunities to engage in mathematical reasoning and sense making in the best mathematics courses that a school district offers. Moreover, each state and school district should identify prerequisite courses that offer students access to rigorous curricula in middle school and high school. Then, examining the apple characteristics of students is usually acceptable to educators as a reasonable and equitable approach to serving the needs of all students. However, educators generally believe that using apple characteristics to determine which students will require remedial mathematics and which students should be given opportunities to take high-track mathematics courses will serve the same students that at-risk models would identify. Educators often feel shocked and unsettled when analysis of objective performance data reveals unexpected outcomes.

For example, in North Carolina, near the end of grade 5, all students take a state standardized EOG assessment in mathematics. A student can score at level I, II, III, or IV. Level I or II indicates students below grade level. Level III indicates students at grade level, and level IV indicates students above grade level. Since an eighth-grade algebra course in North Carolina is arguably the gateway course to rigorous high school mathematics and enhanced opportunities to engage in mathematical reasoning and sense making, failure to be placed into the high track in sixth-grade mathematics represents losing access to rigorous high school mathematics courses (Stiff, Johnson, and Akos, forthcoming). This is true because students rarely gain access to an eighth-grade algebra course if they do not take the high-track sixth-grade mathematics course (O'Connor, Lewis, and Mueller 2007).

Examining the apple characteristics of students in eighth-grade algebra courses in one urban school district in North Carolina revealed that most of them had scored level IV on their grade 5 EOG mathematics test. However, many more students who scored level IV on that assessment did not get the opportunity to take an algebra course in grade 8 because they were not tracked high in sixth-grade mathematics. In fact, fewer than half of the students who scored level IV on their fifth-grade EOG mathematics assessment had the opportunity to study algebra in the eighth grade. Moreover, the percentages of level IV students who were tracked high in sixth-grade mathematics and continued on to study algebra in the eighth grade differed by race and ethnicity at a statistically significant level at a p value of 0.001; see figure 5.2.

These findings occur in many urban and rural school districts across the state. Moreover, the more rural a school district is, or the more rural a school is within a school district, the lower the percentages of level IV students who have an opportunity to take an eighth-grade algebra course. This was especially true for level IV minority students; see figure 5.3.

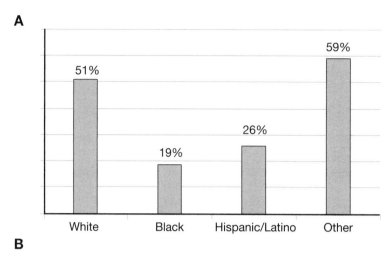

Fig. 5.2. (A) Percentages of level IV students in an urban North Carolina school district who tracked high in sixth-grade mathematics and took algebra in the eighth grade. (B) Numbers of students who tracked high in sixth-grade mathematics by race and ethnicity.

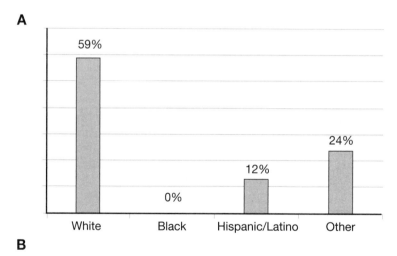

Fig. 5.3. (A) Percentages of level IV students in a rural North Carolina school district who tracked high in sixth-grade mathematics and took algebra in the eighth grade. (B) Numbers of students who tracked high in sixth-grade mathematics by race and ethnicity.

One of the more startling and unsettling outcomes from using pro-equity models is the opportunity that students have (or do not have) to engage in mathematical reasoning and sense making in high-track mathematics courses in the sixth grade. Figure 5.4 describes a common pattern of opportunity for students of different ethnic and racial backgrounds.

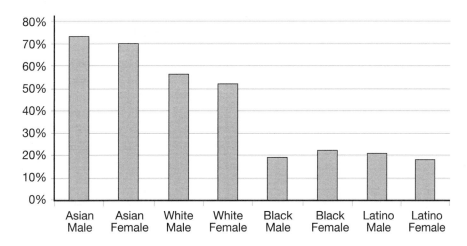

Fig. 5.4. Percentages of sixth-grade level IV math students in an urban North Carolina school district who enrolled into the top track in mathematics

Student achievement is often linked to the financial and human resources that schools command (NCTM 2009). Class size, instructional resources, the number of high-track courses, and teacher salaries reflect the discrepancies between wealthy and poor school districts. Such discrepancies affect the opportunities that students have to excel (Darling-Hammond 2004; Tate and Rousseau 2007). Indeed, a lack of resources adversely affects students' opportunity to participate in Saturday and summer enrichment programs, the quality and experience of teachers, the quality and rigor of school curricula, and teacher turnover rates (Darling-Hammond 2004; Bishop and Forgasz 2007; Education Trust 2008). However, the impact of fewer resources may affect students' opportunity to learn in unexpected ways. Specifically, with existing resources, the implementation of a pro-equity model consistently identifies many students who are well qualified to engage in mathematical reasoning and sense making but are underserved because of a lack of access to high-quality mathematics courses. Such access may be denied because "'at-risk' students are not ready for the high-track mathematics courses." But access is often denied because not enough qualified teachers are available to teach the high-track mathematics courses, or remediation and underachievement, rather than excellence, define the disposition of the school. For the last two explanations, fewer resources often translates into maintaining the at-risk status quo instead of using resources to empower high-performing students and challenge all students to do more.

Whereas at-risk models undervalue students' ability to learn, pro-equity models champion it. But educators hesitate to give more students access unless some objective achievement criteria are established and become the basis for determining which students gain access to high-track mathematics courses. Objective achievement criteria must be acceptable to all parties with a vested interest in who gains access to high-quality mathematics. At a minimum, this category includes mathematics teachers, counselors, and administrators. (Other interested parties include educators in the gifted-and-talented programs and parents.) Many mathematics educators agree to use a pro-equity model because they expect that the number of students who will gain access to high-quality mathematics courses in a pro-equity model will not exceed the number of students that the at-risk model would identify.

Although entire school districts should institute objective achievement criteria, these criteria may vary among school districts. For example, one large urban school district in North Carolina required that students meet two of the following criteria for placement into the top track of sixth-grade mathematics: (1) have a supportive teacher recommendation; (2) score at a high level III or at level IV on the EOG assessment; and (3) receive a grade no lower than a 3 (on a scale of 4) on their standards-based report cards, along with two work samples. However, the attitudes and beliefs that underpin at-risk models continue to prevent many eligible students from gaining the opportunity to participate in high-quality instruction.

For example, one middle school in this large urban school district "overlooked" 103 sixth-grade students who met the placement criteria for the top track in mathematics. After reassignment and placement in the top-track mathematics course, with no additional interventions, students performed consistently with their pro-equity indicators (fig. 5.5). Although advocates of the pro-equity model expected these results, many mathematics teachers expressed utter surprise because these students would have had no opportunity to engage in mathematical reasoning and sense making otherwise.

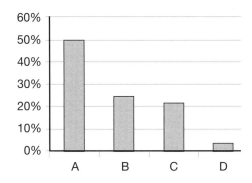

Fig. 5.5. Distribution of course grades for the 103 overlooked students one semester after enrolling in the top-track sixth-grade mathematics course

Any objective achievement criterion will increase the number of students in the high tracks in mathematics and significantly increase the number of minority and low-income students who gain the opportunity to engage in mathematical reasoning and sense making through the top tracks in mathematics. Any pro-equity model that examines service indicators and uses objective achievement criteria to serve the needs of all students gives more students meaningful opportunities in mathematics. Acknowledging this relationship is important because, given the opportunity, students will outperform their at-risk labels (Hoffer, Rasinski, and Moore 1995; Gutiérrez 2000; Education Trust–West 2004; Garrity 2004; Education Trust 2005; Burris, Heubert, and Levin 2006).

Opportunity to Learn and the Need for Systemic Change

All students should have the opportunity to engage in mathematical reasoning and sense making in every course they take: "All too often, teachers' and administrators' views of students' ability, motivation, behavior, and future aspirations are influenced by their beliefs associated with such student identifiers as race, gender, socioeconomic status, native language, and home life. In turn, those beliefs can have serious consequences for the opportunities that a school provides to its students" (NCTM 2009, p. 98). In essence, at-risk models for serving students reinforce teacher dispositions to maintain low expectations for many of the students we serve, and no mantra exhorting "high expectations for all students" can ever replace concrete actions that expect more of students—and teachers. Although exceptions exist, mathematics teachers and mathematics programs seldom offer meaningful opportunities to engage in reasoning and sense making in the low or regular tracks that middle schools—and especially high schools—offer. This assertion is true, in part, because more out-of-field teachers are assigned to teach low- and regular-track classes (Tate and Rousseau 2002). But it is also true because the expectations of low- and regular-track mathematics courses are not high.

In high schools that have multiple levels of the same course (e.g., algebra 1, algebra 1—part 1 and part 2, algebra 1 with technology—part 1 and part 2), students are not likely to have the same or similar experiences for engaging in mathematical reasoning and sense making. Furthermore, students' lack of readiness for algebra cannot be solved by at-risk paradigms that support the expansion of algebra over two years; prealgebra courses for students ready for algebra; or enrichment programs in the summer or after school for students misplaced into remedial, low, or regular classes. Although some students would benefit from algebra offered over two years, prealgebra courses in high school, and enrichment programs, the ranks of these courses are brimming with students who have already demonstrated the ability to do more—students for whom an opportunity lost at the start becomes a cancer to future success.

Pro-equity models do not "overlook" students; they prescribe concrete actions on the basis of student performance and/or objective achievement criteria that lead to high-quality opportunities to learn. More students can engage in mathematical reasoning and sense making, and fewer students are damaged academically because of incorrect assumptions about their abilities. Students who need interventions are properly identified; the likelihood of offering all students better services is enhanced.

Enhanced but not guaranteed: recall the 103 sixth-grade students who were "overlooked" but met the placement criteria for the top track in mathematics in figure 5.5. Although many of these students were previously designated low achieving and behaviorally and emotionally handicapped, these students were nevertheless placed into the top track because the principal of the school insisted that they be given an opportunity to succeed even if the mathematics faculty did not agree about placing these students in the high-performing classes. And, although these students performed well when they had the opportunity to succeed, similar students in the next year's classes did not get the opportunity to engage in mathematical reasoning and sense making because the new principal (the former principal was reassigned to a high school) would not embrace the pro-equity model used previously if the mathematics faculty did not agree. They did not; the results in figure 5.5 were not enough evidence to change their beliefs and attitudes.

Having the opportunity to learn rigorous and important mathematics should not vary from year to year, school to school, in any school district. The goal of every school district must be to create systemic change for implementing pro-equity models for serving the needs of all students. This task is formidable, however. School districts and educators often encounter deeply held beliefs and attitudes about intelligence, racial differences, social class, and privilege that affect efforts to give all students greater opportunity (Oakes and Wells 1998). Special-interest groups in schools and communities have a stake in the status quo, which fuels resistance to any changes in school practices and policies. And affluent parents are not shy about voicing concerns about "equitable policies" that they fear will eliminate opportunities for their children (McGrath and Kuriloff 1999).

Developing strategies for creating change in school systems is vital to offering more opportunities in mathematics for all students. Volumes have been written to address educators' concerns regarding school change. Three pivotal factors have an immediate impact on implementing pro-equity models: (1) school and district policies affecting students' opportunity to learn high-quality mathematics; (2) the quality and nature of mathematics curricula and instruction; and (3) educators' beliefs, attitudes, and dispositions about who can and should engage in learning rigorous mathematics (Welner 2001).

These factors, which are amenable to change, form a fulcrum for student achievement (fig. 5.6). Every pro-equity model examines these three factors to determine how best to serve students. The interconnectedness among these key factors is inherent in the structure of the fulcrum, and although student achievement may depend on other factors in their experiences, these three pivotal factors are central to school-based opportunities.

Student Achievement

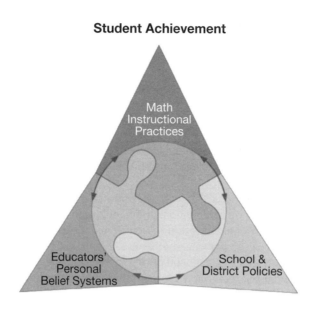

Fig. 5.6. Fulcrum of student achievement

Pro-equity models use data to reconcile the three pivotal factors with the achievement goals of school districts. Each factor may mask roadblocks to engaging students in reasoning and sense making in high-quality mathematics courses. These roadblocks are constructed from the shortcomings of at-risk paradigms. Pro-equity models expose these roadblocks by affording alternative paths to serving the needs of students and fostering student achievement on the basis of data analytics. Data analytics uses sound research to guide school practices and policies; achievement data to align academic services with student needs; and appropriate, well-defined measures of success to evaluate learning and behavioral outcomes.

For example, educators' lack of skills and knowledge about using data is one of the main roadblocks connected to the first pivotal factor, school and district policies. Before data can be used to help students, educators must decide what measures of student performance are acceptable as indicators of student achievement. Then, educators must determine how to collect, maintain, and analyze the data. Often, these data requirements are impediments to changing school practices or policies and thus become a roadblock to any pro-equity model. Since pro-equity models promote using objective achievement criteria for making decisions about student performance and access to high-quality mathematics, any pro-equity model under consideration must incorporate systemwide professional development to help educators learn more about the collection, maintenance, and proper use of data, if required.

Roadblocks tied to the second pivotal factor, the quality and nature of mathematics curricula and instruction, include the role of ninth-grade algebra in high school curricula and the limited supply of middle school teachers prepared to teach algebra. Students taking algebra in the ninth grade are not generally viewed as eligible for future success as defined by participation in the high-track mathematics and sciences courses found in high schools (Stiff, Johnson, and Akos, forthcoming). Moreover, ninth-grade algebra courses are often taught with no intention to engage students in mathematical reasoning and sense making. In fact, when one controls for academic performance, students who take ninth-grade algebra are far less likely to enroll in the most rigorous and challenging mathematics and science classes in high school than are academically similar students who take eighth-grade algebra; this finding is equally true for the highest-performing students in ninth-grade algebra. In the large urban school district cited earlier, a recent review of its enrollment data found that although honors mathematics courses are open to students who do not take eighth-grade algebra, few students who did not take eighth-grade algebra actually enrolled in honors courses, and none of these students took calculus (Haynie 2009).

The role of ninth-grade algebra has not been to put students on the path of high-quality mathematics. At-risk models see ninth-grade students as unprepared to engage in mathematical reasoning and sense making at the highest levels, thus allowing low-track and regular algebra courses to impede students' future opportunities. Because pro-equity models consistently identify well-qualified ninth-grade students who should be offered honors algebra 1 courses but are not, ninth-grade low-track and regular algebra course offerings that do not lead to advanced mathematics are roadblocks. Pro-equity models place a demand on school districts to create honors algebra 1 courses to serve the needs of well-qualified students who have been overlooked under the "at-risk" paradigm. This demand, if met, results in more students' gaining access to mathematical reasoning and sense making in advanced mathematics courses in high school and supports Tate and Rousseau's (2002) observation that the quality and number of mathematics courses taken in high school account for increased student achievement in mathematics.

The limited supply of middle school teachers prepared to teach algebra is another issue affecting the quality and nature of mathematics curricula and instruction. Since pro-equity models use objective achievement criteria to identify students who should take eighth-grade algebra, more students qualify to take algebra 1 in the eighth grade than do typically enroll. The need for more classes in eighth-grade algebra points to a teacher shortage that at-risk models discount but that pro-equity models address. A school district's inability to identify—or its resistance to supplying—more eighth-grade algebra teachers is a significant roadblock to student opportunity and achievement. Pro-equity models offer quantitative evidence of a need to hire additional algebra teachers and/or to conduct professional development to increase the numbers among the existing staff who can offer quality algebra instruction. Because course placements in middle school mathematics usually dictate the types of postsecondary mathematics and science course options available to students, decisions about who takes algebra in middle school become crucial to students' future opportunity to learn (Akos et al. 2007). Failure to provide services to deserving students whose needs have been documented is malpractice. Doing nothing to correct the problem of underserved students must not be permitted. Still, at-risk models thrive because they demand less of students . . . and less of educators.

The third pivotal factor—educators' beliefs, attitudes, and dispositions about who can and should engage in rigorous mathematics—triggers emotionally sensitive roadblocks to pro-equity models. Pro-equity models examine educators' beliefs, attitudes, and dispositions through the lenses of data and existing practices, often revealing embarrassing outcomes that suggest biases toward minority and low-income students' opportunity to learn high-quality mathematics. Although educators usually admit "some awareness" of these inequities, they insist that they are not aware of the magnitude of the problem. This claim is probably true because at-risk models do not question minority and low-income students' placement in low-track and regular mathematics courses. Nevertheless, educational policies and educators' beliefs and attitudes continue to discriminate against minority and low-income students. Akos, Shoffner, and Ellis (2007) reported that "during the middle school years, students may be inequitably distributed among hierarchies of mathematics courses on the basis of race and economic background, becoming increasingly stratified within these tracks" (p. 238). Mayer's (2008) review of the research echoes similar practices in high school. That is, when one controls for academic achievement, non-Asian minority students have less opportunity to enroll in college-preparatory courses than their Asian and white counterparts.

The existence of the preceding roadblocks and others makes it clear that cultural beliefs and attitudes about low-income and minority students play a significant role in how students are placed in mathematics courses in middle school and high school, which affects their opportunity to learn high-quality mathematics and engage in mathematical reasoning and sense making (Mayer 2008).

Many educators resist pro-equity solutions to problems and reinforce the emotional roadblocks of at-risk paradigms because they fear that to do otherwise would reveal existing inequities that may be attributed to intentional neglect and racial biases. But educators must overcome this fear and use data analytics to make good choices for all the students we serve.

Rejecting what is easy and doing what is right takes leadership. For too long, at-risk models have promoted low expectations. Now we must promote high expectations . . . in concrete ways: we must implement pro-equity models for serving the needs of all students.

References

Abu El-Haj, Thea Renda, and Beth C. Rubin. "Realizing the Equity-Minded Aspirations of Detracking and Inclusion: Toward a Capacity-Oriented Framework for Teacher Education." *Curriculum Inquiry* 39 (June 2009): 435–63.

Akey, Theresa M. *School Context, Student Attitudes and Behavior, and Academic Achievement: An Exploratory Analysis.* New York: MDRC, 2006.

Akos, Patrick, Glenn W. Lambie, Amy Milsom, and Kelly Gilbert. "Early Adolescents' Aspirations and Academic Tracking: An Exploratory Investigation." *Professional School Counseling* 11 (October 2007): 57–64.

Akos, Patrick, Marie Shoffner, and Mark Ellis. "Mathematics Placement and the Transition to Middle School." *Professional School Counseling* 10 (February 2007): 238–44.

Bandura, Albert. "Self-Efficacy." In *Encyclopedia of Human Behavior,* edited by Vilayanur S. Ramachaudran, pp. 71–81. New York: Academic Press, 1994.

Bishop, Alan, and Helen Forgasz. "Issues in Access and Equity in Mathematics Education." In *Second Handbook of Research on Mathematics Teaching and Learning,* edited by Frank K. Lester Jr., pp. 1145–68. Charlotte, N.C.: Information Age Publishing and National Council of Teachers of Mathematics, 2007.

Burris, Carol Corbett, Jay P. Heubert, and Henry M. Levin. "Accelerating Mathematics Achievement Using Heterogeneous Grouping." *American Educational Research Journal* 43 (Spring 2006): 105–36.

Burris, Carol Corbett, and Kevin G. Welner. "Closing the Achievement Gap by Detracking." *Phi Delta Kappan* 86 (April 2005): 594–98.

Callahan, Rebecca M. "Tracking and High School English Learners: Limiting Opportunity to Learn." *American Educational Research Journal* 42 (Summer 2005): 305–28.

Darling-Hammond, Linda. "The Color Line in American Education: Race, Resources, and Student Achievement." *Dubois Review* 1 (September 2004): 213–46.

Darling-Hammond, Linda, Barnett Berry, and Amy Thoreson. "Does Teacher Certification Matter? Evaluating the Evidence." *Education Evaluation and Policy Analysis* 23 (Spring 2001): 57–77.

Education Trust. *Gaining Traction, Gaining Ground: How Some High Schools Accelerate Learning for Struggling Students.* Washington, D.C.: Education Trust, 2005.

———. *Core Problems: Out-of-Field Teaching Persists in Key Academic Courses and High-Poverty Schools.* Washington, D.C.: Education Trust, 2008.

Education Trust–West. *The A–G Curriculum: College Prep? Work Prep? Life Prep: Understanding and Implementing a Rigorous Core Curriculum for All.* Oakland, Calif.: Education Trust–West, 2004.

Garrity, Delia. "Detracking with Vigilance: By Opening the High-Level Doors to All, Rockville Centre Closes the Gap in Achievement and Diplomas." *School Administrator* 61 (August 2004): 24–27.

Goldhaber, Dan D., and Dominic J. Brewer. "Does Teacher Certification Matter? High School Teacher Certification Status and Student Achievement." *Education Evaluation and Policy Analysis* 22 (Summer 2000): 129–45.

Gray, Jeremy R., Todd S. Braver, and Marcus E. Raichle. "Integration of Emotion and Cognition in the Lateral Prefrontal Cortex." *Proceedings of the National Academy of Sciences of the United States of America* 99 (March 2002): 4115–20.

Gutiérrez, Rochelle. "Advancing African American Urban Youth in Mathematics: Unpacking the Success of One Math Department." *American Journal of Education* 109 (November 2000): 63–111.

Hallinan, Maureen T. "Ability Group Effects on High School Learning Outcomes." Paper presented at the 95th annual meeting of the American Sociological Association, Washington, D.C., August 2000.

———. "Ability Grouping and Student Learning." *Brookings Papers on Education Policy, 2003* (2003): 95–124. DOI: 10.1353/pep.2003.0005.

Haynie, Glenda. *High School Mathematics Course-Taking Patterns of Middle School Algebra I Students* (WCPSS E & R Report No. 08.31). Raleigh, N.C.: Wake County Public School System, 2009.

Hoffer, Thomas B., Kenneth A. Rasinski, and Whitney Moore. *Social Background Differences in High School Mathematics and Science Coursetaking and Achievement* (NCES 95-206). National Center for Education Statistics. Washington, D.C.: U.S. Department of Education, 1995.

Jamar, Idorenyin, and Vanessa R. Pitts. "High Expectations: A 'How' of Achieving Equitable Mathematics Classrooms." *Negro Educational Review* 56 (July 2005): 127–34.

Johnson, Janet L., Bernice Campbell, Rita Lewis, Julie Johnson, Marty Redington, and Aniko Gaal. *North Carolina's School Counseling Program Review: A Statewide Survey and Comprehensive Assessment (Vol. 2006)*. Raleigh, N.C.: EDSTAR, 2005.

Kozol, Jonathan. *Savage Inequalities: Children in America's Schools.* New York: Harper Perennial, 1991.

Laczko-Kerr, Ildiko, and David C. Berliner. "The Effectiveness of 'Teach for America' and Other Undercertified Teachers on Student Academic Achievement: A Case of Harmful Public Policy." *Education Policy Analysis Archives* 10 (September 2002). epaa.asu.edu/epaa/v10n37.

Lubienski, Sarah T., and Michele D. Crockett. "NAEP Findings Regarding Race and Ethnicity: Mathematics Achievement, Student Affect, and School–Home Experiences." In *Results and Interpretations of the 2003 Mathematics Assessment of the National Assessment of Educational Progress*, edited by Peter Kloosterman and Frank K. Lester Jr., pp. 227–60. Reston, Va.: National Council of Teachers of Mathematics, 2007.

Mallery, James L., and Janet G. Mallery. "The American Legacy of Ability Grouping: Tracking Reconsidered." *Multicultural Education* 7 (Fall 1999): 13–15.

Mayer, Anysia. "Understanding How U.S. Secondary Schools Sort Students for Instructional Purposes: Are All Students Being Served Equally?" *American Secondary Education* 36 (Spring 2008): 7–25.

McGrath, Daniel J., and Peter J. Kuriloff. "'They're Going to Tear the Doors Off This Place': Upper-Middle-Class Parent School Involvement and the Educational Opportunities of Other People's Children." *Educational Policy* 13 (November 1999): 603–29. DOI: 10.1177/0895904899013005001.

National Council of Teachers of Mathematics (NCTM). *Principles and Standards for School Mathematics.* Reston, Va.: NCTM, 2000.

———. *Focus in High School Mathematics: Reasoning and Sense Making.* Reston, Va.: NCTM, 2009.

O'Connor, Carla, Amanda Lewis, and Jennifer Mueller. "Researching Black Educational Experiences and Outcomes: Theoretical and Methodological Considerations." *Educational Researcher* 36 (December 2007): 541–52.

Oakes, Jeannie, and Amy Stuart Wells. "Detracking for High Student Achievement." *Education Leadership* 55 (March 1998): 38–41.

Peske, Heather G., and Kati Haycock. *Teaching Inequality: How Poor and Minority Students Are Shortchanged on Teacher Quality.* Washington, D.C.: Education Trust, 2006.

Pintrich, Paul R., and Dale H. Schunk. "The Role of Expectancy and Self-Efficacy Beliefs." In *Motivation in Education: Theory, Research, and Applications*, pp. 67–104. Englewood Cliffs, N.J.: Prentice-Hall, 1996.

Schwartz, Wendy. "Teaching Science and Mathematics to At-Risk Students." *Equity and Choice* 4 (Winter 1988): 39–45.

Stiff, Lee V., and William B. Harvey. "On the Education of Black Children in Mathematics." *Journal of Black Studies* 19 (December 1988): 190–203.

Stiff, Lee V., Janet L. Johnson, and Patrick Akos. "Examining What We Know for Sure: Tracking in Middle Grades Mathematics." In *Connecting Research, Practice, and Policy in Mathematics Education,* edited by William Tate, Karen King, and Celia Rousseau Anderson. Reston, Va.: National Council of Teachers of Mathematics, forthcoming.

Stone, Carolyn B., and Robert Turba. "School Counselors Using Technology for Advocacy." *Journal of Technology in Counseling* 1.1 (October 1999). jtc.colstate.edu/vol1_1/advocacy.htm.

Tate, William F., and Celia K. Rousseau. "Access and Opportunity: The Political and Social Context of Mathematics Education." In *Handbook of International Research in Mathematics Education,* edited by Lyn D. English, pp. 271–99. Mahwah, N.J.: Lawrence Erlbaum Associates, 2002.

Tufte, Edward R. *The Visual Display of Quantitative Information.* 2nd ed. Cheshire, Conn.: Graphics Press, 2001.

Vanfossen, Beth E., James D. Jones, and Joan Z. Spade. "Curriculum Tracking and Status Maintenance." *Sociology of Education* 60 (April 1987): 104–22.

Welner, Kevin G. *Legal Rights, Local Wrongs: When Community Control Collides with Educational Equity. SUNY Series, Restructuring and School Change.* Albany, N.Y.: SUNY Press, 2001.

Wheelock, Anne. *Crossing the Tracks: How "Untracking" Can Save America's Schools.* New York: The New Press, 1992.

Yonezawa, Susan, Amy Stuart Wells, and Irene Serna. "Choosing Tracks: 'Freedom of Choice' in Detracking Schools." *American Educational Research Journal* 39 (Spring 2002): 37–67.

Chapter 6

Mathematics Learning Communities That Foster Reasoning and Sense Making for All High School Students

Marilyn E. Strutchens, Judith Reed Quander, and Rochelle Gutiérrez

In an effort to explain the disparities that exist among racial and socioeconomic groups, Flores (2007) reframed the achievement gap as an "opportunity gap," calling attention to the fact that African American and Latina/Latino students are less likely than white students to have teachers who emphasize high-quality mathematics instruction and make appropriate use of resources. For example, African American and Latina/o students are less likely than white students to have access to teachers who emphasize reasoning and nonroutine problem solving and teachers who use computers for simulations and applications rather than for drill and practice (Strutchens and Silver 2000).

In 2000, across the nation, the percentages of twelfth-grade white, African American, and Latina/o students who reported taking algebra 1 in the ninth grade, geometry in the tenth grade, and algebra 2 in eleventh grade were not significantly different; however, white students were significantly more likely than African American or Latino students to report taking precalculus in twelfth grade (15%, 10%, and 10%, respectively; Strutchens et al. [2004]). According to Tate and Rousseau (2007), "the two most powerful predictors of school mathematics achievement in large-scale assessments of mathematics have been (a) increased time on task in high-level mathematics and (b) the number of courses taken in mathematics" (p. 1221). In fact, between African American and white students who completed the same number of mathematics courses, the difference in average achievement gains was smaller than in other circumstances, and none was statistically significant (Hoffer et al. 1995). Moreover, Asian and white students' mathematics achievement gains were smaller and generally reduced among students completing the same number of mathematics courses (Hoffer et al. 1995). Furthermore, none of the comparisons by socioeconomic status (SES) showed significant differences among students taking the same number of courses (Hoffer et al. 1995; Tate 1998). Therefore, Tate (1998) concluded that the findings by Hoffer and colleagues (1995) "could be interpreted to mean that much of the racial and SES differences in mathematics achievement in grades 9–12 can be attributed to the different numbers of mathematics courses that African American and white, Asian and white, and high- and low-SES students complete during secondary school" (pp. 135–36). These claims are consistent with the results from the 2005 twelfth-grade mathematics assessment for the National Assessment of Educational Progress, which showed that taking higher-level mathematics courses was associated with higher mathematics scores (Lee, Grigg, and Dion 2007). In fact, some studies have suggested that if students took algebra in the eighth grade, they were more likely to complete advanced courses in high school, regardless of parents' level of education (Horn, Bobbitt, and NCES 2010). In particular, students who completed mathematics beyond algebra 2 substantially increased their chances of enrolling in a four-year college.

Thus, equity issues are at the core of students' pathways to college or mathematical fields. Lipman (2004) contended that the concept of equity includes "the equitable distribution of material and human resources; intellectually challenging curricula; educational experiences that build on students' cultures, languages, home experiences, and identities; and pedagogies that prepare students to engage in critical thought and democratic participation in society" (p. 3). This definition aligns with *Rising above the Gathering Storm* (CSEPP 2007), which stated that improvements in student achievement are solidly linked to teacher excellence, characterized by thorough knowledge of content, solid pedagogical skills, motivational abilities, and career-long opportunities for continuing education. The report continued that "excellent teachers inspire young people to develop analytical and problem-solving skills, the ability to interpret information and communicate what they learn, and ultimately to master conceptual understanding" (CSEPP 2007, p. 113).

Other researchers have suggested that equity is achieved only when we cannot predict student achievement; rates of participation in mathematics; students' abilities to see themselves reflected in and through the curriculum; and engagement in meaningful problem solving in one's community simply by knowing students' ethnic, racial, religious, cultural, linguistic, or gendered backgrounds (Gutiérrez 2002a). Gutiérrez (1999) declared, "If we intend to take seriously the National Council of Teachers of Mathematics' goal of *mathematics for all,* we must better understand not only the practices and beliefs of culturally relevant teachers, but how individuals come together to create culturally relevant teaching communities" (p. 265). One part of the puzzle seems to be school cultures and teachers that support marginalized students in taking many mathematics courses and more advanced classes than is typically the case. How some schools accomplish this goal is important for understanding how other schools might follow suit.

Researchers who have examined schools that serve primarily African Americans, Latinas/os, and low-income whites document features common to effective mathematics departments (producing gains in students' achievement over time) and absent in departments that are ineffective (with little, no, or negative gains on students' achievement): a rigorous and common curriculum, active commitment to students, commitment to a collective enterprise, and innovative instructional practices that include respecting and attending to students' linguistic and cultural needs (Gutiérrez 1996, 1999, 2000, 2002b, 2007). Teachers in other studies, such as at Railside High School, echo the evidence of these effective practices: "The mathematics teachers at Railside achieved something important that many other teachers could learn from—they organized an effective instructional program for students from traditionally marginalized backgrounds, and they taught students to enjoy mathematics and to include it as part of their futures" (Boaler and Staples 2008, p. 610).

The success story of Railside highlights how (1) the pedagogy used by the teachers in the school led to "relational equity"—that is, students' learning to treat each other equitably and showing respect for students of different cultures, genders, and social classes; (2) the mathematics department worked together as a team and had a common vision and culture; (3) the instructors taught classes with the principles of complex instruction, which addressed student status issues; and (4) the math department designed the curriculum and pulled ideas from National Council of Teachers of Mathematics (NCTM) Standards–based mathematics programs. In this chapter, we examine the role of the teacher collective and its importance in helping more students to develop reasoning and sense-making skills related to mathematics, to have their cultures and languages valued, and to stay in the mathematics pipeline.

What Can Mathematics Departments Do to Foster More Students' Success in Mathematics?

Beyond just working side by side in the same hallway, holding regularly scheduled meetings, and forming collegial bonds over teaching similar subjects, high school mathematics departments offer collegiality, motivation, and opportunities for reflection for practicing teachers. Also, the high school mathematics department can make real change in a school. An entire department focused on one goal, such as increasing the number of African American high school students taking advanced mathematics (Gutiérrez 2000), increasing the number of bilingual Latina/o students taking calculus (Gutiérrez 2002b), or detracking the mathematics program (Horn 2006), can be a powerful force in a high school. Further, the department chairperson can be a major influence on the teachers in a department—supporting progress toward a goal of change, such as the one described in *Focus in High School Mathematics: Reasoning and Sense Making* (NCTM 2009). Strong teacher leaders know that they must ask themselves the following kinds of questions:

- Are we doing enough to engage teachers and their students in meaningful ways that draw on their passions and future goals?

- If we have achieved some success, can we do things differently so that we can get even more teachers and their students on board?

- By whose standards are we achieving success? (Gutiérrez, Bay-Williams, and Kanold 2008)

Looking across these studies reveals that ensuring the success of more students in high school mathematics requires several important department-wide behaviors, including having a rigorous curriculum focused on college-preparatory mathematics that all high school students must take; support for students so that they can succeed; teachers with strong commitment and high expectations for students; and innovative teaching practices to help teachers reach all students.

Union High School

Gutiérrez (1999, 2002b) reported on Union High School, an inner-city school with a relatively poor and culturally and linguistically diverse student population, a predominantly white and middle-class staff, and few resources. The members of Union's mathematics department were a combination of veterans (more than five years' experience at the school) and newly hired teachers with a variety of preferred teaching styles. A self-defined social activist chaired the mathematics department. As chair, he used his power to promote policies and teaching practices that supported many students in mathematics, partly through including and motivating faculty. Specifically, he advocated for teachers' rights to determine both the curriculum and the most appropriate approaches for teaching.

The core of the teacher collective at Union High School was developed through a partnership between the school and a university, during the 1990–1995 academic years (Gutiérrez 1999; Gutiérrez and Morales 2002). This partnership offered, among other things, release time (one additional preparatory period), training in cooperative learning, new teachers with similar beliefs about students, and opportunities to discuss how best to support students. The training sessions led to community building and trust among the mathematics teachers that served as a foundation for the student advancement they experienced. From the teachers' discussions of how best to support students came their desire and determination to advance more students to higher levels of mathematics. At first, teachers worked with the highest-performing students—ones who would be taking trigonometry or calculus regardless of the school setting. Eventually, these teachers broadened their definition of who should take calculus, and to date, they encourage any students who show moderate skill levels by their junior year to continue into calculus.

Although the school required only two years of mathematics for graduation, members of the mathematics department persuaded many students to take calculus by their senior year. All students at Union High took algebra in their freshman year and geometry in their sophomore year. Also, as juniors, students were encouraged to take advanced algebra/trigonometry and an intensive, six-week college algebra course (over the summer). Furthermore, in their senior year, these students took a double period of calculus to prepare for the Advanced Placement exam.

Persuading students to enroll in upper-level courses was only part of the story that led to the teachers' success with students. Union High School teachers worked together with the students to support them in several ways. The teachers collaborated with each other in ways that moved the students forward mathematically, understood the students as complex sociocultural beings and considered home cultures and languages when making instructional decisions, and spent time with students beyond regular class time to help them with their studies. The teachers sought professional development in the College Preparatory Mathematics Program, which emphasized effective use of cooperative groups, and in the Interactive Mathematics Program (IMP), which helped students to reason and make sense of mathematics. They also recruited and socialized new members into their department who shared their philosophy about mathematics. In fact, the department's commitment to the kind of sense-making problems that the IMP curriculum offered—which prepared students for success in calculus—meant that teachers continued to create and incorporate similar problems in grades 9–11 even after their school district decided to eliminate the IMP courses.

Students at Union High took more mathematics courses than the required two for graduation, with approximately 40 percent of the senior class taking calculus. Moreover, the students who were enrolled in calculus classes reflected the general student population at this comprehensive high school (including English learners, members of gangs, recent immigrants, and qualifiers for free and reduced-price lunch). These students attended college at rates that far surpassed those of their peers in other schools. Teachers and students alike attributed the kinds of instructional practices and student success at Union to a community of teachers who valued and supported students' advancing in mathematics (Gutiérrez 2002b).

Key elements of the teacher community at Union High include the following:

- Developing and sharing instructional materials (e.g., collectively developing lesson plans, performing formal and informal assessments, valuing both veteran and novice teachers' contributions)

- Communicating and reflecting on students and instruction (e.g., focusing instruction on particular students, raising questions about how particular students or classes are doing, debating what the goals of instruction should be)

- Reinforcing the belief that all students can learn calculus (e.g., discussing how lower levels of mathematics relate to calculus, sharing success stories)

- Planning for classes inside and outside school (e.g., holding meetings at teachers' homes and during preparatory periods, conducting conference calls)

- Rotating course assignments (e.g., sharing lower-level and higher-level courses each year, including placing newer teachers in the highest-level classes)

- Placing students and their needs at the center of their work (e.g., viewing their position as teachers of students first and of mathematics second, emphasizing students' ownership of the mathematics and the calculus program)

- Visiting one another's classrooms (e.g., sharing how a particular worksheet or quiz worked with a given set of students that teachers had in previous years) (Gutiérrez and Morales 2002, p. 232)

Monterey High School

Monterey High School, a predominantly African American, lower-class to lower-middle-class school in urban Maryland, is another example of a mathematics department successful in supporting its student population to take more and higher levels of mathematics than their peers at comparable schools (Gutiérrez 2000). Much of that success was attributed to the school's mathematics department, which consisted of teachers with various levels of experience, with some new to the school and others new to teaching altogether. Five departmental activities account for this teacher community's success: (1) offering a rigorous, common curriculum with little stratification, along with the necessary support for student success; (2) being available to students; (3) holding a common commitment to students and each other, with a focus on a shared goal; (4) having a chair who served as both a facilitator and a resource for the department; and (5) adopting instructional practices aligned with NCTM's recommendations for teaching.

The mathematics department at Monterey worked together and instituted departmental policies, all in the name of success for their students (Gutiérrez 2000). All students at Monterey took a college-preparatory curriculum with a variety of courses offered, from algebra 1 to calculus, with all students taking algebra 1 their freshman year. Even further, the faculty in the department chose to support a district measure to get rid of non–college-preparatory courses, such as consumer mathematics, where schools often place weaker students and that do not prepare students for college. Committed to a strong mathematics program for their students, the mathematics department lobbied to keep advanced mathematics courses that the district was looking to terminate. Also, whereas the district required students to graduate with geometry, Monterey instituted a three-course minimum. This policy, coupled with all students' taking algebra 1 as freshmen, resulted in most students' completing algebra 1, geometry, and algebra 2 while in high school.

To help even those students with weak backgrounds in mathematics succeed in courses such as algebra 1, the department offered students a great deal of support. For example, students who enrolled in algebra 1, but who had not performed well on state tests, could take a yearlong laboratory class taught simultaneously with algebra 1 that reviewed foundational topics for students. This measure limited the time that algebra 1 teachers spent reviewing previous course material.

In addition to making sure that students had access to rigorous mathematics and support to succeed, the teachers made themselves accessible to their students—tutoring before and after school and sometimes on weekends. The teachers' high expectations and beliefs in their students' chances for success fueled their push for a strong curriculum and their willingness to help their students outside the school day. The teachers in this department spoke positively about their students and looked for students' strengths as opposed to buying into stereotypes about what African American students can and cannot do and what interests them. When teachers think that their students can do meaningful mathematics, teachers realize that their role is to support the students to succeed. At Monterey, this support happened through after-school tutoring, weekend workshops, and general accessibility.

In many high schools, seniority determines the courses that a teacher teaches. That is, the most veteran teachers might get the upper-level courses, whereas the newer teachers are assigned the lower-level courses, sometimes referred to as "teacher tracking." At Monterey, the mathematics department rotated courses so that all teachers in the department had the chance to teach a variety of courses over their careers. This approach had a lot of input and negotiation from the teachers. Although sometimes it caused extra work for the teachers (prepping for multiple courses), overall the teachers felt that this approach to scheduling benefited the students (faculty developed a sense of responsibility to all students), as well as the teachers themselves (teachers learned to recognize and make greater connections between mathematical topics and courses such as algebra and calculus). For one, changing courses meant that the teachers had to actively seek professional development to help them teach courses that were new to them. Also—although not explicitly described in the study of Monterey but present in Union's mathematics department—in a rotating approach to scheduling, experienced teachers are not strictly teaching courses such as precalculus and calculus. They are teaching lower-level mathematics courses, which undoubtedly benefits students in those courses, who are sometimes thought of as mathematically weak. Beyond working together to figure out scheduling, Monterey teachers described their department as collaborative and working together regularly to achieve the common goal of having more students take higher-level mathematics.

Probably the most powerful indication of its commitment to the students was the department's willingness to adapt its teaching practices to meet students' needs. Recognizing that mathematics instruction cannot be "one size fits all," Monterey teachers described the various approaches they used to make mathematics more accessible to their students—many of which NCTM's various Standards supported. The teachers placed less emphasis on drilling and rote memorization and relied more on cooperative learning, technological tools, knowledge construction, and real-world problems (Gutiérrez 2000)—components that featured prominently in the *Curriculum and Evaluation Standards for School Mathematics* (NCTM 1989). Students solved problems similar to example 10 from *Focus in High School Mathematics: Reasoning and Sense Making* (NCTM 2009):

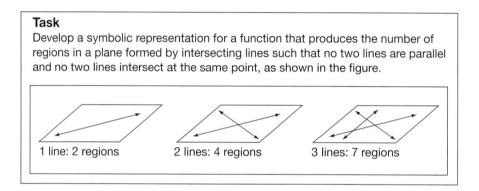

Task
Develop a symbolic representation for a function that produces the number of regions in a plane formed by intersecting lines such that no two lines are parallel and no two lines intersect at the same point, as shown in the figure.

1 line: 2 regions   2 lines: 4 regions   3 lines: 7 regions

Teachers afforded students the opportunity to solve problems like this one in a variety of ways, such as looking for patterns and using technology. See *Focus in High School Mathematics: Reasoning and Sense Making* for possible solutions.

Moreover, the teachers wanted to ensure that all students had the opportunity to learn important mathematics; they described using technology flexibly to help students with weak arithmetic skills engage in more complex mathematics. Other instructional approaches incorporated cooperative group work into classes and related mathematics to students' lives by incorporating their interests in mathematics lessons.

Although one cannot say that the Monterey math department's strong collaborative spirit and their even stronger commitment to student success actually caused their students to be more successful in mathematics, one cannot deny their students' success. That their department's activities did not contribute in some major way seems unlikely. The students at Monterey performed better on tests than did peers, attended college at more significant rates, and took more and higher levels of mathematics than peers at other schools.

East High School

A different study found similar traits in a mathematics department that successfully detracked its high school mathematics program (Horn 2006). Although several approaches to detracking exist, the mathematics department of East High School, located in an urban setting with a diverse student population, had revamped its entire organizational structure so that all entering freshmen took the same college-preparatory mathematics class their first year of high school. Similar to Union and Monterey high schools, students at East High School (especially those often underrepresented in science, technology, engineering, and mathematics–related classes) took more advanced mathematics and had a higher success rate than their peers in other schools. Students at East High School also reported having positive feelings about mathematics and about themselves as learners of mathematics. Also, because of their push for reforming the mathematics program, the faculty members in the mathematics department at East High School were considered leaders in the school.

Some of the qualities and specific behaviors that contributed to East's ability to successfully detrack its mathematics program included the following:

- Teachers' understanding mathematics as a connected and complicated subject
- Employing a mathematics curriculum focused on important and meaningful mathematics
- Striking a balance between individual and coordinated decision making
- Directly addressing what "doing school" versus "doing mathematics" means

Imperative to successfully detracking a mathematics program is the belief that all students, regardless of past mathematics experiences and ability levels, can succeed even in higher levels of mathematics. Although mathematics is traditionally seen as a linear progression in a well-established hierarchy, the teachers in the mathematics department at East High School did not regard mathematics in this way. This view has important consequences for how mathematics is taught and the learning opportunities offered to students. For example, if you believe that mathematics is linear, then you might say that students cannot engage in algebraic reasoning until they have mastered basic facts. However, at East High, the teachers described mathematics as interrelated ideas that connect to each other in important ways. The goal for mathematics teaching and learning is for students to make sense of what they are doing. The teachers believed that with suitable scaffolding and support from teachers, students of all ability levels could understand mathematical ideas. Also, with this concept of teaching mathematics, the phrase *good at math* had new meaning. The students were not expected to quickly move through pages of problems or to memorize algorithms; instead, these classrooms valued understanding and making sense of mathematical concepts. Students who could solve problems—not by mindless manipulation but through careful and sophisticated reasoning—were held in high esteem.

Therefore, East High School had an innovative approach to its curriculum, an approach defined as focusing the curriculum on group-worthy problems. The department "collectively defined group-worthy problems as having four distinctive properties; they: (a) illustrated important mathematical concepts, (b) included multiple tasks that drew effectively on the collective resources of a student group, (c) allowed for multiple representations, and (d) had several possible solution paths" (Horn 2006, p. 76). The following is an example of one problem from an algebra class:

> *The Vending Machine.* In this problem, students were told about the daily consumption patterns of soda in a factory's vending machine, including when breaks were, when the machine got refilled, and the work hours in the factory. Students were then asked to make a graph that represented the number of sodas in the vending machine as a function of the time of day. The activity focused on one larger problem organized around a set of constraints. Although these constraints limited the possible answers, students had an opportunity to discuss the different choices that would satisfy the constraints and look for common features of plausible solutions as a way of generalizing the mathematical ideas. Embedded in the activity were important mathematical ideas (graphing change, slope, rate) that were linked to a real-world context. (Horn 2006, p. 76)

Curricular units were also arranged around big ideas and included contextual situations to help students relate the mathematics that they were learning to their lives.

East High School's mathematics department collaboratively defined a vision for mathematics teaching and learning on the basis of a complex view of mathematics. The teachers agreed on a curriculum focused on important mathematics and centered on group-worthy mathematics problems. However, in a detracked classroom—with a variety of learning abilities and attainment levels—one can imagine that reaching each student requires a great deal of adaptation. Even though subjects in the department had a common curriculum, the teachers of East High School had to depend on their own discretion to make decisions about scaffolding and appropriate timing of tasks, among others. However, Horn described a strong focus on cooperation and collaboration within the department, with the ultimate goal of student success. Because courses were completed in semesters—two semesters per year—students could have as many as seven mathematics teachers in high school. Therefore, the department touched base often about students. In particular, at the beginning of each semester, the teachers met to discuss one another's course roster for the semester, focusing on high-risk students. Teachers gave feedback regarding successful strategies that they had used with these students to help guide the current teacher's instructional approaches. Regular course meetings also took place to discuss, among other pertinent topics, adapting textbook materials to fit teachers' view of mathematics teaching and learning. In general, the department members used one another as resources and built time into their workweek for collaboration.

Finally, understanding that being a good student is often tied to conforming to certain norms and expectations, the mathematics department at East High School addressed this need in its students directly. For example, completing homework is an expectation of students. Therefore, at the front of each classroom was a homework chart with a grid of students' names and homework assignment titles, where teachers recorded whether students completed assignments. Although completing an assignment is not explicitly linked to mathematics learning, it is an important part of being a student. Such support systems were put in place to help students reach expectations. However, although the teachers did emphasize the importance of supporting students in being students, teachers did not confuse being a student or not being a student with the ability to learn. For example, if a student did not finish his or her homework regularly, this did not mean that the student could not be good in mathematics; rather, he or she needed additional support and time to succeed in a traditional schooling environment.

Railside, Union, Monterey, and East High are all examples of high schools with mathematics departments whose faculty decided to raise the mathematics achievement and engagement levels of all their students. All these mathematics departments had similar characteristics: (1) effective mathematics learning communities (teacher collectives); (2) more advanced-level courses than low-level courses, with expectations that students will matriculate through the courses well; and (3) teachers who used pedagogical strategies aimed at engaging all students in learning meaningful mathematics.

Components of Effective Mathematics Departments for All Students

The following sections take a closer look at these school mathematics departments' common elements.

Mathematics learning community (teacher collective)

Much of what has occurred at these and similar schools is the result of a commitment by the mathematics faculty to work together to develop mathematical learning communities that are effective for their respective student populations and their surrounding communities. A mathematics learning community can be a cross between a professional community—a community where "teachers participate in decision making, have a shared sense of purpose, engage in collaborative work and accept joint responsibility for the outcomes of their work" (Harris 2003, p. 321)—and a learning community that engages students, teachers, administrators, and other stakeholders simultaneously in learning (Hord 1997). The mathematics departments discussed in the preceding section are mathematics learning communities at the intersection of professional communities and learning communities. The departments contained infrastructures that supported collaboration and created internal and external conditions for mutual learning (Harris 2003). Moreover, Gutiérrez (1999) stated the following about the teachers at Union High:

Merely requiring teachers to work together on curriculum materials or spend more hours with their students is an insufficient condition for creating a teaching culture conducive to Latina/o student advancement. In fact, teachers need time—time to meet, time to develop themselves, and time to create momentum. We see that Union's partnership with a local university for the purposes of curriculum reform catalyzed a much broader agenda. The release time they were granted was a critical piece of their success. Without this additional support, teachers are unlikely to find the time to have the meaningful conversations about mathematics, students, and education that were the basis of the trust they built. Without a strong foundation of trust, teachers will have a hard time opening their classroom doors or their personal lives to others—a process that seems to have a positive outcome for teachers *and* students.

Not only do teachers need time to develop themselves and their work as effective collectives, they need ongoing support from administration for the kinds of teaching and relationships that support students. Core teachers report they could accomplish even greater advancement with students if they worked more closely with other department members. (p. 276–77)

More than simply time for planning and learning with other teachers, essential components for establishing and sustaining a professional community include expanding notions of resources to include human and social resources (Farnsworth 2002). These resources are essential for teachers to (1) share a sense of purpose, (2) focus collectively on student learning, (3) collaborate on ways to improve student learning, (4) engage in reflective dialogue on the nature and practice of teaching, and (5) make public their own teaching practice. The mathematics departments at Railside, Union, Monterey, and East High showed what is possible when teachers truly develop strong mathematics learning communities in which their goals are to move all students forward and keep them in the mathematics pipeline.

Rigorous curriculum with expectations for all students to succeed

Another hallmark of the aforementioned effective mathematics departments is their offering more advanced-level courses than lower-level courses, with expectations that students will matriculate through the courses well. The mathematics teachers of Railside, Union, Monterey, and East High wanted their students to reach their full mathematics potential. Thus, the faculty offered a greater proportion of upper-level mathematics courses than lower-level courses and supported students to reach their expectations. And the teachers often taught a variety of courses. No one teacher was responsible for the upper-level courses each semester; the faculty rotated the responsibilities so that each teacher could experience teaching algebra 1 through calculus, where appropriate. Rotating responsibility for courses is unusual in high schools. Some schools reward more-effective teachers by assigning them to the higher tracks; in other schools, seniority or teacher choice governs course and track-level assignments (Hallinan 1994). Also, according to Jeannie Oakes, teachers who are most likely to be assigned to low-track classes are the least experienced; those without teaching credentials; and, at the secondary level, those with the lowest levels of preparation in their fields (O'Neil 1992). Moreover, teachers who have the most confidence in their abilities are often assigned to the high-track courses (O'Neil 1992). Some researchers have even suggested the following:

Low-income students and students of color suffer disproportionately from these negative effects, both because they are tracked disproportionately into the lowest classes in racially mixed schools and because they are more likely to attend racially isolated schools where lower-level classes predominate. Through tracking, schools continue to replicate existing inequality along lines of race and social class and contribute to the intergenerational transmission of social and economic inequality. And for all the hand wringing over the "achievement gap," schools continue to promote low achievement for poor children, African Americans, Latinos, and other underserved groups by placing these students disproportionately in "low" classes. (Oakes 2008, p. 705)

Thus, offering students more opportunities to take upper-level courses and strategically placing teachers in courses that challenge students to reason and make sense of mathematics are laudable and necessary components to increase the number of students who stay in the mathematics pipeline and go into related fields.

Pedagogical strategies aimed at engaging all students in learning meaningful mathematics

The third salient attribute of these effective mathematics departments is teachers who used pedagogical strategies aimed at engaging all students in learning meaningful mathematics. All the aforementioned departments emphasized using particular pedagogical strategies aimed at helping students to reason and make sense of mathematics, such as aligning practices with NCTM Standards (NCTM 1989, 1991, 1995, 2000), using cooperative learning groups (Cohen et al. 1999), and applying culturally relevant practices (Ladson-Billings 1994, 1995a, 1995b).

The NCTM Standards movement, which began with *Curriculum and Evaluation Standards for School Mathematics* (NCTM 1989), encouraged changes in mathematics teaching and learning, especially around including all students, using technologies, alternative forms of assessment, and the need for increased professional development and other key issues of practice. In support of the 1989 Standards, the National Science Foundation (1995) initiated curricular development of standards-based materials that differed from traditional textbook materials. These materials tended to incorporate, by design, more problems set in realistic contexts; accepted fewer exercises requiring only arithmetic or algebraic manipulations; required more use of calculators and computers; and encouraged teachers to pose problems to solve by using various strategies, to organize students to work in small groups, and to work with heterogeneously grouped classes (Senk and Thompson 2003). Many teachers in the aforementioned mathematics departments used some of the NCTM Standards–based curriculum materials and had experienced success; their students became more engaged in doing mathematics, and student achievement increased.

In keeping with the use of NCTM Standards–based curriculum materials, most teachers in the effective mathematics departments used some form of cooperative learning—one of the teaching strategies that NCTM (2008, 2009) advocates. The "Actions for Teachers" section of the NCTM Position Statement on Equity asks teachers to "organize ways to provide students with the opportunity to work in different groups and have a chance to take on different roles in the group." Moreover, *Focus in High School Mathematics: Reasoning and Sense Making* (NCTM 2009) states, "Effective instruction requires having and communicating high expectations for all students. In such learning environments, students continually explore interesting tasks, either individually or in groups, and communicate their conjectures and conclusions to others. Pedagogical techniques and carefully designed instructional materials further ensure that the focus of instruction is on students' thinking and reasoning, and provide opportunities for all students to participate" (p. 103).

In agreement, many teachers in the effective high school mathematics departments featured here used complex instruction. Complex instruction is a form of cooperative learning in which students are assigned open-ended, interdependent group tasks and serve as academic and linguistic resources for each other, and their teacher addresses status issues to ensure that all students have the opportunity to be heard and to participate well (Cohen et al. 1999). When using this approach, the teacher should be involved in the following activities: (1) observing the pupils; (2) listening to the discussions in the groups at a proper distance; (3) interjecting key questions to groups that are stuck; (4) giving individuals and groups positive feedback; (5) watching for who is participating and who is not and the reasons for this; and (6) reminding the groups about rules, roles, and norms (Kujansivu and Rosell 2000). See chapter 1 in this book for a discussion of complex instruction's other benefits for students.

Culturally relevant teaching was another strategy that teachers in the effective mathematics departments used (Ladson-Billings 1994, 1995a, 1995b). The major components of culturally relevant teaching include the following:

1. Teachers work to help their students better understand what racism is, how it works, and what they can do to work against it.

2. Students treated as competent are likely to demonstrate competence.

3. Giving students instructional scaffolding allows them to move from what they know to what they do not know.

4. The major focus of the classroom must be instructional.

5. Real education is about extending students' thinking and ability beyond what they already know.

6. Effective pedagogical practice involves in-depth knowledge of students as well as subject matter (Ladson-Billings 1994, 1995a).

If implemented correctly, these components can lead to students' (1) experiencing academic success, (2) developing and/or maintaining cultural competence, and (3) developing a critical consciousness through which they challenge the status quo of the current social order (Ladson-Billings 1995b). The mathematics departments mentioned earlier used various configurations of culturally relevant teaching. The faculty members in the departments worked hard to get to know their students beyond stereotypes or essential categories and to move their students forward academically.

Per NCTM Standards–based practices, using cooperative learning and culturally relevant teaching strategies was one component of the effective mathematics departments' success. Implementing these strategies helped the faculty members to engage their students in mathematical learning situations that were meaningful and motivational. Through their pedagogy, the teachers helped the students not only to stay in the mathematics pipeline by taking upper-level mathematics courses, but also to use mathematics as a way to understand their world.

Conclusion

We presented information on four successful mathematics departments to show the importance of the teacher collective. Even though individual teachers make a difference, educators can achieve more when all members of a mathematics department have the same goal of helping all students to engage in meaningful mathematics that leads to more productive career options. The components of the effective mathematics departments that we highlighted are (1) effective mathematics learning communities (teacher collectives); (2) more advanced-level courses than low-level courses, with expectations that students will matriculate through the courses well; and (3) teachers who used pedagogical strategies aimed at engaging all students in learning meaningful mathematics. If these components are in place in more school mathematics departments, more students are likely to become successful mathematics learners.

References

Boaler, Jo, and Megan Staples. "Creating Mathematical Futures through an Equitable Teaching Approach: The Case of Railside School." *Teachers College Record* 110 (January 2008): 608–45.

Cohen, Elizabeth G., Rachel A. Lotan, Beth A. Scarloss, and Adele R. Arellano. "Complex Instruction: Equity in Cooperative Learning Classrooms." *Theory into Practice* 38 (Spring 1999): 80–86.

Committee on Science, Engineering, and Public Policy (CSEPP). *Rising above the Gathering Storm: Energizing and Employing America for a Brighter Economic Future.* Washington, D.C.: National Academies Press, 2007.

Farnsworth, Valerie. "Supporting Professional Development and Teaching for Understanding—Actions for Administrators." *In Brief* 2 (Fall 2002). ERIC Document Reproduction no. ED470964.

Flores, Alfinio. "Examining Disparities in Mathematics Education: Achievement Gap or Opportunity Gap?" *High School Journal* 91 (October 2007): 29–42.

Gutiérrez, Rochelle. "Practices, Beliefs, and Cultures of High School Mathematics Departments: Understanding Their Influence on Student Advancement." *Journal of Curriculum Studies* 28 (September 1996): 495–529.

———. "Advancing Urban Latina/o Youth in Mathematics: Lessons from an Effective High School Mathematics Department." *Urban Review* 31 (September 1999): 263–81.

———. "Advancing African American Urban Youth in Mathematics: Unpacking the Success of One Math Department." *American Journal of Education* 109 (November 2000): 63–111.

———. "Enabling the Practice of Mathematics Teachers in Context: Toward a New Equity Research Agenda." *Mathematical Thinking and Learning* 4 (July 2002a): 145–87.

———. "Beyond Essentialism: The Complexity of Language in Teaching Mathematics to Latina/o Students." *American Educational Research Journal* 39 (Winter 2002b): 1047–88.

———. "Context Matters: Equity, Success, and the Future of Mathematics Education." Paper presented at the annual meeting of the North American Chapter of the International Group for the Psychology of Mathematics Education, Reno, Nev., October 2007.

Gutiérrez, Rochelle, Jennifer Bay-Williams, and Timothy D. Kanold. "Moving Beyond Access and Achievement: What Should Mathematics Teachers and Leaders Consider When Addressing Equity Issues?" *NCTM News Bulletin.* Reston, Va.: National Council of Teachers of Mathematics, 2008.

Gutiérrez, Rochelle, and Hector Morales. "Teacher Community, Socialization, and Biography in Reforming Mathematics." In *Reforming Chicago's High Schools: Research Perspectives on School and System Level Change,* edited by V. E. Lee and A. Bryk, pp. 223–49. Chicago: Consortium on Chicago School Research, 2002.

Hallinan, Maureen T. "Tracking: From Theory to Practice." *Sociology of Education* 67 (April 1994): 79–84.

Harris, Alma. "Teacher Leadership as Distributed Leadership: Heresy, Fantasy or Possibility?" *School Leadership and Management* 23 (August 2003): 313–24.

Hoffer, Thomas B., Kenneth A. Rasinski, Whitney Moore, and the National Opinion Research Center. "Statistics in Brief: Social Background Differences in High School Mathematics and Science Coursetaking and Achievement." 1995. nces.ed.gov/pubsearch/pubsinfo.asp?pubid=95206 (accessed August 31, 2010).

Hord, Shirley M. "Professional Learning Communities: What Are They and Why Are They Important?" *Issues about Change* 6, no. 1 (1997). www.sedl.org/change/issues/issues61.html (accessed December 28, 2009).

Horn, Ilana Seidel. "Lessons Learned from Detracked Mathematics Departments." *Theory into Practice* 45 (January 2006): 72–81.

Horn, Laura, Larry Bobbitt, and National Center for Education Statistics (NCES). "Mapping the Road to College: First-Generation Students' Math Track, Planning Strategies, and Context of Support. Statistical Analysis Report. Postsecondary Education Descriptive Analysis Reports." March 2000. nces.ed.gov/pubs2000/2000153.pdf (accessed September 1, 2010).

Kujansivu, Arja, and Jan-Åke Rosell. "Complex Instruction as a Tool for Developing the Role of the Teacher. A Workshop Presented at the 'Intercultural Education and Co-Operative Learning' Conference in Ghent, May 2000." *Intercultural Education* 11 (Suppl. 1, December 2000): 21–26.

Ladson-Billings, Gloria. *The Dreamkeepers: Successful Teachers of African American Children.* San Francisco: Jossey-Bass, 1994.

———. "Making Mathematics Meaningful in Multicultural Contexts." In *New Directions for Equity in Mathematics Education,* edited by Walter Secada, Elizabeth Fennema, and Lisa Byrd Adjian, pp. 126–45.

New York: Cambridge University Press, 1995a.

———. "But That's Just Good Teaching! The Case for Culturally Relevant Pedagogy." *Theory into Practice* 34 (Summer 1995b): 159–65.

Lee, Jihyun, Wendy S. Grigg, and Gloria S. Dion. *The Nation's Report Card: Mathematics 2007* (NCES 2007-494). U.S. Department of Education. Washington, D.C.: National Center for Education Statistics, 2007.

Lipman, Pauline. *Regionalization of Urban Education: The Political Economy and Racial Politics of Chicago-Metro Region Schools.* Paper presented at the annual meeting of the American Educational Research Association, San Diego, April 2004.

National Council of Teachers of Mathematics (NCTM). *Curriculum and Evaluation Standards for School Mathematics.* Reston, Va.: NCTM, 1989.

———. *Professional Standards for Teaching Mathematics.* Reston, Va.: NCTM, 1991.

———. *Assessment Standards for School Mathematics.* Reston, Va.: NCTM, 1995.

———. *Principles and Standards for School Mathematics.* Reston, Va.: NCTM, 2000.

———. "Equity in Mathematics Education." January 2008. www.nctm.org/about/content.aspx?id=13490 (accessed September 12, 2010).

National Science Foundation. "Instructional Materials Development, Fiscal Years 1991–1994. Summary of Awards." Arlington, Va.: National Science Foundation, 1995. ERIC Document Reproduction no. ED395824.

O'Neil, John. "On Tracking and Individual Differences: A Conversation with Jeannie Oakes." *Educational Leadership* 50 (October 1992): 18–21.

Oakes, Jeannie. "Keeping Track: Structuring Equality and Inequality in an Era of Accountability." *Teachers College Record* 110, no. 3 (2008): 700–12.

Senk, Sharon L., and Denisse R. Thompson, eds. *Standards-Based School Mathematics Curricula: What Are They? What Do Students Learn?* Mahwah, N.J.: Lawrence Erlbaum Associates, 2003.

Strutchens, Marilyn E., Sarah Thuele Lubienski, Rebecca McGraw, and Sarah K. Westbrook. "NAEP Findings Regarding Race/Ethnicity: Students' Performance, School Experiences, Attitudes and Beliefs, and Family Influences." In *Results and Interpretations of the 1990 through 2000 Mathematics Assessments of the National Assessment of Educational Progress*, edited by Peter Kloosterman and Frank K. Lester Jr., pp. 269–304. Reston, Va.: National Council of Teachers of Mathematics, 2004.

Strutchens, Marilyn E., and Edward A. Silver. "NAEP Findings Regarding Race/Ethnicity: The Students, Their Performance, and Their Classrooms." In *Results from the Seventh Mathematics Assessment of the National Assessment of Educational Progress*, edited by Edward A. Silver and Patricia A. Kenney, pp. 45–72. Reston, Va.: National Council of Teachers of Mathematics, 2000.

Tate, William F. "Stating the Obvious: Mathematics Course Taking Matters." In *The Nature and Role of Algebra in the K–14 Curriculum: Proceedings of a National Symposium (Washington, DC, May 27–28, 1997)*, edited by the National Academy of Sciences, National Research Council, Mathematical Sciences Education Board, and the National Council of Teachers of Mathematics, pp. 152–53. Washington, D.C.: National Academies Press, 1998. ERIC Document Reproduction no. ED429801.

Tate, William F., and Celia K. Rousseau. "Engineering Change in Mathematics Education: Research, Policy, and Practice." In *Second Handbook of Research on Mathematics Teaching and Learning*, edited by Frank K. Lester Jr., vol. 2, pp. 1209–45. Charlotte, N.C.: Information Age Publishing and National Council of Teachers of Mathematics, 2007.

Appendix

The Equity Principle

The Equity Principle

Excellence in mathematics education requires equity—high expectations and strong support for all students.

Making the vision of the *Principles and Standards for School Mathematics* a reality for all students, prekindergarten through grade 12, is both an essential goal and a significant challenge. Achieving this goal requires raising expectations for students' learning, developing effective methods of supporting the learning of mathematics by all students, and providing students and teachers with the resources they need.

Educational equity is a core element of this vision. All students, regardless of their personal characteristics, backgrounds, or physical challenges, must have opportunities to study—and support to learn—mathematics. Equity does not mean that every student should receive identical instruction; instead, it demands that reasonable and appropriate accommodations be made as needed to promote access and attainment for all students.

Equity is interwoven with the other Principles. All students need access each year to a coherent, challenging mathematics curriculum taught by competent and well-supported mathematics teachers. Moreover, students' learning and achievement should be assessed and reported in ways that point to areas requiring prompt additional attention. Technology can assist in achieving equity and must be accessible to all students.

Equity requires high expectations and worthwhile opportunities for all.

The vision of equity in mathematics education challenges a pervasive societal belief in North America that only some students are capable of learning mathematics. This belief, in contrast to the equally pervasive view that all students can and should learn to read and write in English, leads to low expectations for too many students. Low expectations are especially problematic because students who live in poverty, students who are not native speakers of English, students with disabilities, females, and many nonwhite students have traditionally been far more likely than their counterparts in other demographic groups to be the victims of low expectations. Expectations must be raised—mathematics can and must be learned by *all* students.

The Equity Principle demands that high expectations for mathematics learning be communicated in words and deeds to all students. Teachers communicate expectations in their interactions with students during classroom instruction, through their comments on students' papers, when assigning students to instructional groups, through the presence or absence of consistent support for students who are striving for high levels of attainment, and in their contacts with significant adults in a student's life. These actions, along with decisions and actions taken outside the classroom to assign students to different classes or curricula, also determine students' opportunities to learn and influence students' beliefs about their own abilities to succeed in mathematics. Schools have an obligation to ensure that all students participate in a strong instructional program that supports their mathematics learning. High expectations can be achieved in part with instructional programs that are interesting for students and help them see the importance and utility of continued mathematical study for their own futures.

Equity requires accommodating differences to help everyone learn mathematics.

Higher expectations are necessary, but they are not sufficient to accomplish the goal of an equitable school mathematics education for all students. All students should have access to an excellent and equitable mathematics program that provides solid support for their learning and is responsive to their prior knowledge, intellectual strengths, and personal interests.

Some students may need further assistance to meet high mathematics expectations. Students who are not native speakers of English, for instance, may need special attention to allow them to participate fully in classroom discussions. Some of these students may also need assessment accommodations. If their understanding is assessed only in English, their mathematical proficiency may not be accurately evaluated.

Students with disabilities may need increased time to complete assignments, or they may benefit from the use of oral rather than written assessments. Students who have difficulty in mathematics may need additional resources, such as after-school programs, peer mentoring, or cross-age tutoring. Likewise, students with special interests or exceptional talent in mathematics may need enrichment programs or additional resources to challenge and engage them. The talent and interest of these students must be nurtured and supported so that they have the opportunity and guidance to excel. Schools and school systems must take care to accommodate the special needs of some students without inhibiting the learning of others.

Technology can help achieve equity in the classroom. For example, technological tools and environments can give all students opportunities to explore complex problems and mathematical ideas, can furnish structured tutorials to students needing additional instruction and practice on skills, or can link students in rural communities to instructional opportunities or intellectual resources not readily available in their locales. Computers with voice-recognition or voice-creation software can offer teachers and peers access to the mathematical ideas and arguments developed by students with disabilities who would otherwise be unable to share their thinking. Moreover, technology can be effective in attracting students who disengage from nontechnological approaches to mathematics. It is important that all students have opportunities to use technology in appropriate ways so that they have access to interesting and important mathematical ideas. Access to technology must not become yet another dimension of educational inequity.

Equity requires resources and support for all classrooms and all students.

Well-documented examples demonstrate that all children, including those who have been traditionally underserved, can learn mathematics when they have access to high-quality instructional programs that support their learning (Campbell 1995; Griffin, Case, and Siegler 1994; Knapp et al. 1995; Silver and Stein 1996). These examples should become the norm rather than the exception in school mathematics education.

Achieving equity requires a significant allocation of human and material resources in schools and classrooms. Instructional tools, curriculum materials, special supplemental programs, and the skillful use of community resources undoubtedly play important roles. An even more important component is the professional development of teachers. Teachers need help to understand the strengths and needs of students who come from diverse linguistic and cultural backgrounds, who have specific disabilities, or who possess a special talent and interest in mathematics. To accommodate differences among students effectively and sensitively, teachers also need to understand and confront their own beliefs and biases.

References

Campbell, Patricia. *Project IMPACT: Increasing Mathematics Power for All Children and Teachers.* Phase 1, Final Report. College Park, Md.: Center for Mathematics Education, University of Maryland, 1995.

Griffin, Sharon A., Robbie Case, and Robert S. Siegler. "Rightstart: Providing the Central Conceptual Prerequisites for First Formal Learning of Arithmetic to Students at Risk for School Failure." In *Classroom Lessons: Integrating Cognitive Theory and Classroom Practice*, edited by Kate McGilly, pp. 25–49. Cambridge, Mass.: MIT Press, 1994.

Knapp, Michael S., Nancy E. Adelman, Camille Marder, Heather McCollum, Margaret C. Needels, Christine Padilla, Patrick M. Shields, Brenda J. Turnbull, and Andrew A. Zucker. *Teaching for Meaning in High-Poverty Schools.* New York: Teachers College Press, 1995.

Silver, Edward A., and Mary Kay Stein. "The QUASAR Project: The 'Revolution of the Possible' in Mathematics Instructional Reform in Urban Middle Schools. *Urban Education* 30 (January 1996): 476–521.

Ti Jacques
A STORY OF HAITI

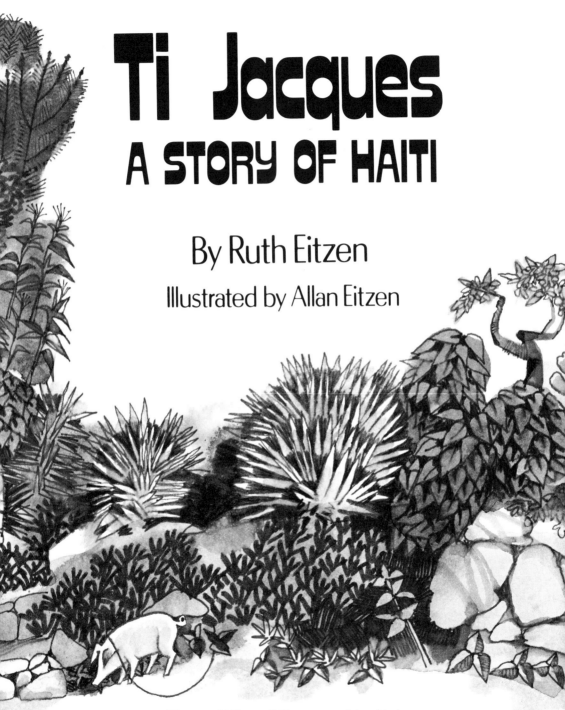

Ti Jacques
A STORY OF HAITI

By Ruth Eitzen

Illustrated by Allan Eitzen

Thomas Y. Crowell Company · New York

STORIES FROM MANY LANDS

THE GOATS WHO KILLED THE LEOPARD: A STORY OF ETHIOPIA
By Judy Hawes

THE GREEN, GREEN SEA: A STORY OF GREECE
By Molly Cone

THE HOUSE IN THE TREE: A STORY OF ISRAEL
By Molly Cone

MAKOTO, THE SMALLEST BOY: A STORY OF JAPAN
By Yoshiko Uchida

THE MEETING POST: A STORY OF LAPLAND
By Lee Kingman

MIKA'S APPLE TREE: A STORY OF FINLAND
By Clyde Robert Bulla

THE MOST TERRIBLE TURK: A STORY OF TURKEY
By Joseph Krumgold

NEW BOY IN DUBLIN: A STORY OF IRELAND
By Clyde Robert Bulla

THE ROAD TO KATMANDU: A STORY OF NEPAL
By Arnold Dobrin

TI JACQUES: A STORY OF HAITI
By Ruth Eitzen

THE TWO HATS: A STORY OF PORTUGAL
By Roland Bertol

Manufactured in the United States of America
L.C. Card 76-158688
ISBN 0-690-82429-7
(LIB. ED. 0-690-82430-0)
1   2   3   4   5   6   7   8   9   10

To the Turnbulls who showed us the real Haiti

Across the deep and distant valley, Godet Mountain was pink with dawn. Ti Jacques' whole family was up. Their breakfast of hot coffee warmed them against the chilly morning breeze. Vitale helped heave a big basket of yams onto Ti Jacques' head.

"Quick, Ti Jacques!" called Mama. Her own basket was already balanced. She was leaving for market. Vitale could not resist a parting jab in the ribs of his older brother. "Mama's girl!" he whispered.

Ti Jacques trotted jauntily down the rocky path. He wasn't afraid of a girl's job like carrying a yam basket, not if it took him to Port-au-Prince, the largest city in Haiti. He was only afraid that some market day his brother would get the job instead of him.

He jogged quickly past his father, Gro Jacques, already limping to the corn patch. "There goes Ti Jacques, strutting like a rooster," commented his father. "What kind of trouble are you going to get us into today?"

Ti Jacques glanced at his father to see if he was laughing. He was not. A thought flew through Ti Jacques' head like the shadow of a blackbird: "Papa wishes he were going to the city himself!"

Ti Jacques could remember how his father used to keep him proudly by his side as he crouched by the cooking fire. "Ti moun," he would say, "little man, you have your father's name; may you have his strength and wisdom." Then he would laugh and see that Little Jacques got the choicest morsel from the cooking pot. But that was long ago. It was when Big Jacques still had a strong back and two good legs. It was before he got hit by a taxi. He was still a guide then, showing travelers the sights of Port-au-Prince. It seemed a long, long time since those days.

"Papa has many worries," said Ti Jacques' mother after they had walked for some time.

"What would he have to worry about?" asked Ti Jacques, surprised.

"For one thing, he's worried you'll get into trouble, with all your nosiness." Ti Jacques looked astonished. He had already forgotten the scoldings

2

of the past. "Take care, Ti Jacques. Papa's accident lost us our cornfield. Just one more piece of bad luck, and next we'll have no home at all."

"Oh, never, Mama!" Ti Jacques assured her. Nothing was more secure to him than their thatched home in the banana grove. Gro Jacques had fashioned it from sticks and mud with his own hands. And Ti Jacques was as sure of their garden plot as he was of the Haitian mountains.

"Ti Jacques," his mother cautioned him, "a donkey walks in a donkey's tracks."

"You are right, Mama, what happened once could happen again," Ti Jacques admitted. "But you forget one thing. I am strong!"

"Yes, son," said Mama, laughing a little, "but I am not sure how wise you are."

When at last they reached the marketplace, the sun was golden as a grapefruit. The warm air was sour-sweet with the smells of purple soap, overripe mangoes, and crisp, sizzling porky grillo. It was a day for Ti Jacques, made for him. He liked things big, and that was market day in Port-au-Prince— big noise, big crowds, big commotion. By noon they had sold enough so that Mama could go and buy some sugar, salt, and cooking oil.

"You promised us pork fat this time, Mama," Ti Jacques reminded her. He was hungry enough by now to enjoy a raw yam.

"We get the pork fat if we sell the yams," said Mama. "I am going to leave you in charge of that. Don't run around snooping. Stay right here and sell all you can."

"Don't worry, Mama. I'll take care of every-thing," said Ti Jacques. All the same she looked back once more to say, "Remember now!"

Why did she worry like that? Ti Jacques began right away to call to the passersby in a loud voice, "Fine yams! Fine fat yams! Fine, fat, fresh yams!" As he yelled, he watched.

Eiya! That fellow over there must have at least twenty hats on his head. And he's trying to sell one to a man with a shoulder bag.

"Eight gourdes!" he says.

"Robbery! I'll give you three," shouts the man with a bag.

"Eight! Oh, well, I'll make a gift to you for six."

"Four gourdes, that's the top!"

"Six!"

"Four!" The hatman shook his head emphatically, and all the hats shook with it. In disgust he pushed off among the crowd, muttering, "What does he expect, a Christmas present?"

Madame Polo under her banana leaf lean-to did not seem to be doing much better. Her printed feed bags flapped gaily in the breeze, but her wrinkled face was sour as a week-old lemon. Business was not great today, but Ti Jacques was sure he could make some good sales. Then for a raspberry ice at the fresco cart! His mouth watered at the thought. Or a hot cassava cake! His stomach, hollow all morning, began to growl with anticipation.

"Yams! Good and cheap!" he cried. An old lady came his way, dragging a squealing pig. As she went by, she stepped square on his toes, and so did the pig.

Above the usual buzz and clatter of the market, Ti Jacques heard a long, low hiss. Behind him, not far away, a car stopped, and its passengers got out,

excited and upset. No wonder. They were foreigners, and ladies at that. Ti Jacques ran over to have a look, keeping one eye on his yams. The ladies had run over broken glass, their tire was ruined, and they did not know what to do.

Nosy as he was, Ti Jacques had seen how flat tires were changed. There were plenty of flats on the rough, stony roads. "Those poor souls need a hand," thought Ti Jacques. "With no trouble I can help them and still keep one eye on the yams."

Ti Jacques went over to the ladies and cranked his arm up and down vigorously beside the wheel of the car to show what he could do. It's lucky for them I'm so strong! he was thinking. The ladies talked among themselves. After considerable rummaging in the trunk among bags and big straw hats, they found a jack and a spare tire. Ti Jacques smiled to himself as he set the jack in place. How could rich people with a car be so ignorant? He was thinking of an old saying he had heard: Being stupid doesn't kill a Haitian, it just makes him sweat. He saw it held true of foreigners too.

Ump! This job was not as easy as it looked. Ti

Jacques dropped the nuts in the hubcap and
struggled to get the new tire in place. That took
effort.

He set the wrench in place on the nuts and
tugged them tight. Ciyé! Ti Jacques wiped his

9

hands on his pants. The job was done; the old cut tire lay in the street.

Ti Jacques could use that tire. He pointed out its gashes to the lady behind the wheel, who was reaching in her handbag. "Shall I get that old beat-up tire out of the way?" he said in Creole, forgetting she couldn't understand. He motioned from the tire to himself. The lady laughed, thanked him in queer French, and gave him the tire. She also paid him three coins for changing it.

Thoughtful as Ti Jacques was being, there was one thought he had forgotten. Yams! He rushed toward his basket, rolling the tire in front of him. From here everything looked just as he had left it. But when he got closer, he saw. The yams were gone. No sign of them anywhere.

Mama's eyes shone when she returned and saw the empty basket. "Ti Jacques! To think you could get rid of all those yams so fast! Wait till Papa hears!"

"Mama," said Ti Jacques, getting up slowly from the tire on which he was sitting. "I don't know how to tell you this. I had to help some

ladies in distress. I wasn't far. I was keeping an eye on the yams, but . . . ."

"Ti Jacques!" was all Mama said. Then she put her basket on her head and started for home. There was nothing in it now but sugar, salt, and cooking oil. There was nothing in Ti Jacques' basket at all. Pork fat was not to be had for three little coins.

"I'm sorry, Mama," Ti Jacques said sadly.

But as the tire bumped along up the mountain trail with him behind it, Ti Jacques began to cheer up. He had big ideas for this tire. It was to be a surprise for Gro Jacques. Papa always liked to be making something, if he had something to make it with.

From this tire Papa could make maybe ten pairs of strong sandals. Everybody in Port-au-Prince needed sandals. They were not to be seen walking barefoot in the city. That was the law. Near home at last, Ti Jacques hid the tire in the banana grove.

Supper that night was not very gay and not very filling. Vitale fished around in the cooking pot among the corn meal and beans. He all but stuck his head in the pot, looking for something.

11

"Where is the pork fat you promised?" he asked
Mama.

"It was a bad day at market, a bad one," replied
Mama.

Gro Jacques looked suspiciously at Ti Jacques.
"Did the bad market have something to do with
that one?" he asked, nodding his head in Ti
Jacques' direction. Mama stirred the beans busily.

"Yes," said Papa. "It has something to do with
that one. He stays home next time. He is bad luck
at the market."

12

Ti Jacques was very much ashamed, and still hungry. Worse, he felt the sad hungry eyes of Mama, Papa, and Vitale looking at him, the nosy, worthless one, and thinking about pork fat. He disappeared into the banana grove.

There was a thumping and bumping, and Ti Jacques was back again, with the tire. "Papa," he said hopefully, "I am presenting you with a surprise."

"Humph! You can't eat an old tire," grumbled Vitale. Mama gave him a smack.

13

"I haven't had my hands on one of these for years," Papa laughed. "It'll make a good stew when I'm through with it." It was true. The strong sandals Papa would make would bring enough money for pork fat, and for pork, too.

There was a lot to do before the next market day. The boys were to help with the work, and they always started out well enough. But if the morning brought a donkey clopping down the trail, Ti Jacques would forget everything and run to see who it was and where they were going. At the slightest stir in the banana grove, Vitale too would be gone, looking for a bird or animal. Then he would take charcoal and draw what he had seen on the big rock behind their hut. And if in the cool of the evening the boys heard the drums in the village near their home, they knew it was Papa, and surely you must go and dance when it is your papa who beats the drums.

Mama would sigh and just work all the harder. "Bon Dieu bon," she would sometimes murmur. "God must know what he is doing to give me three men like this."

14

Sometimes Papa would say, "Why do you work so hard? Tomorrow a storm will come and wash the garden all away." This had happened often enough, but they knew that if Mama really did stop working it might very well be the end of them.

Papa was good at making anything, even music, but he was not much of a farmer, especially since the accident. Now as his row of finished sandals grew longer and longer, his mood grew better and better. He was almost his old self.

Ti Jacques looked at it this way: "When Papa's not working, he is ashamed to see Mama working so hard." Yes, he was sure his papa and Vitale felt just as he did. He could tell by the way they started out working in the field in the morning. Strong and bold, like brave soldiers out to slay the enemy. But long after each of them had disappeared, Mama's old broken hoe still clicked and clacked among the stones. The big rock was full of pictures; the evenings were full of drum songs; and Ti Jacques' head was full of ideas. Each of them was strong at something, but usually only Mama was strong at doing what had to be done.

However, this was a good week. When market day came, there were not only yams and beans but also ten pairs of sandals to take to Port-au-Prince.

"Take Vitale along this time," said Papa. "The boys can keep each other out of mischief." So the three of them went down the mountain path, Mama swaying like a queen with the big basket of yams on her head, Ti Jacques carrying the sandals in pairs over his shoulder, and Vitale with the beans.

After they had sold some sandals in the market, Mama let the boys go down to the center of the city to peddle. "Be careful to start home early," she warned them, "so Tonton Macoute doesn't get you."

The boys took her words to heart, since they were afraid of the dark and of Tonton Macoute, the old bogeyman with a basket for carrying off boys.

Off the brothers went, down the hill toward the center of town. The dome of the President's palace shone through the trees in the park. A tall white cathedral with a cross in the middle towered over

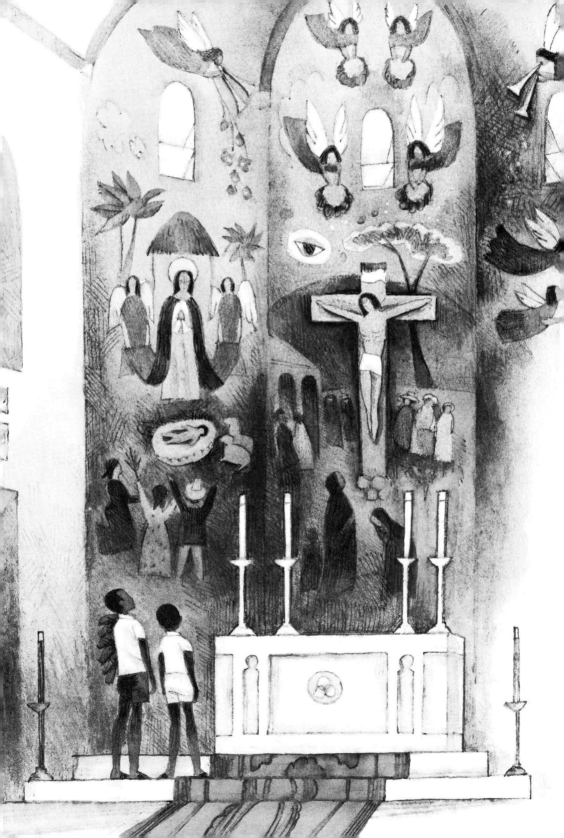

the palm trees. This was the church where Papa
used to take tourists.

"I'll take you in," said Ti Jacques, leading the
way through the iron gate of the courtyard. Since
the front door was locked, he poked around the
side of the building.

"Do you really think we should be here?"
asked Vitale.

"Yes. Oh, sure. No doubt about it," his brother
reassured him, as he reached a heavy back door,
slightly ajar. "What's God's is everybody's."

Before they knew it, the boys were in a great
high place. Above, the dome was like an April
sky. Around it bright painted angels flew, blowing
trumpets and carrying garlands. Haitians like
themselves gathered about the Saviour's cross. On

19

one side shepherds and sheep painted as large as life knelt before a brown baby in a basket of rushes. The boys stood in quiet amazement in this world so full of mystery and yet so familiar.

Suddenly there was a thud. Ti Jacques' papa's sandals had slipped to the floor. The boys recalled with a start what they were supposed to be doing. They tiptoed quickly through the church and came out into a courtyard framed with arches and balconies. From these came the sound of children singing. Exploring down an alleyway, they came upon a room open to the sky, with red-flowered flame trees growing from the paved floor. Pots of paints in all colors stood around, and boys and girls were sitting everywhere on the floor, singing and painting pictures.

A sister in a long robe of gray and white came in, and the boys started to run. The sister caught Ti Jacques' sleeve. "What's the hurry?" she asked. "Stay and pay us a visit."

She gave each of them a brush and a large piece of paper. Vitale took the brush and began to paint as if he painted every day of his life. He was

20

making a flame tree full of birds. There were few birds in Haiti, but here Vitale could paint as many as he wanted. Ti Jacques was busy mixing colors on his paper to find out what would happen. As he leaned back to admire his work, a bell rang.

Ti Jacques and Vitale remembered for the first time that they had forgotten again! They jumped up to leave. The sister told them to come again. "And until then," she said, "here is something for you." Into the boys' hands she put a brush and a few used jars of paint.

The boys went down the street carrying their paintings like furled flags. Vitale, bearing the paints and brush, felt as if he had just found treasure. But as they walked down the hill, they began to have some worries. It was afternoon, and there were still the sandals to sell.

"Look!" Ti Jacques shouted, pointing down-hill over the rooftops. "A cruise ship is in!" He grabbed Vitale's arm and began to hurry toward the harbor where the ship was putting down anchor.

Vitale pulled away. "What?" he called after his brother. "With all these sandals?"

"Oh, come on. We don't see a cruise ship every day," argued Ti Jacques. "We'll sell to the tourists."

"Do foreigners wear this kind of sandals?" asked Vitale.

"Well, no. But maybe when they see these, they'll begin," Ti Jacques told him. "Papa should be here now!"

"Why can't Papa be a guide anyway?" Vitale questioned his brother as he gave in and followed

him down the hill. "It's not that he can't walk."

"Fellows with good legs get there first. Too many guides and not enough tourists these days," explained Ti Jacques. Vitale was too young to remember much, but Ti Jacques remembered how Papa had limped to the city again and again, and come back sad and angry.

When the boys got to the harbor, guides were already crowded around waiting for the passengers. No chance to sell sandals here. "Clear out!" they growled, shoving the boys out of the way.

The gangplank went down then, and people began to pour out of the ship. Their bright new bags and colorful clothes gleamed in the sun. The guides rushed forward, each wanting to be first. Without thinking, Ti Jacques thrust his sandals into Vitale's hand and hustled forward too. He was thin and quick, and it was easy for him to slip between the grown men. He found himself in the midst of a tourist family.

In a minute, Ti Jacques became a porter, trotting side by side with the children of the family, carrying bags. He glanced at Vitale and motioned

him to follow. On the way to the hotel, another, even better idea was hatching in Ti Jacques' head. Papa could show this family around the city to-morrow! As he gave them their bags and got his pay, he said, "Guide? Guide?"

The father looked at his family. "Yes," he re-plied. "Wednesday."

That was tomorrow. Jubilant as a runaway goat, Ti Jacques found his brother. "Good news, Vitale!" he shouted.

"It looks like bad news to me," answered Vitale.

He held up the unsold sandals with a frown. His shadow lay along the pebbled ground like a worried echo of himself. It was already late. If they did not sell the sandals, there was Papa to be afraid of. In any case there was Tonton Macoute, the bogeyman, and Loo Garoo, the werewolf, to fear.

If Ti Jacques was afraid, he did not show it. "Papa won't have a word to say about these sandals, when he hears the news," said Ti Jacques with his usual bravado. "Not a word!"

Vitale asked no questions. He was running as if Tonton Macoute was not far behind. Ti Jacques' big ideas were all right for daylight. But they wouldn't do a bit of good when it got dark. If it came to a choice between Tonton Macoute, Loo Garoo, and an angry Papa, he'd take Papa.

Uphill the boys ran, stopping from time to time to get their breath. Ti Jacques' sides hurt, so he spit on a stone and threw it over his shoulder.

All the time the mountains were getting more ghostly, and the last light was sifting away. There was not time even to get a drink at the waterfall. The miles home from the city had never been so long.

When the boys flopped down at last by their own banana grove, it was almost dark. They couldn't even speak when Mama found them, the unsold sandals still on their shoulders.

"Where have you been this time?" she asked, looking the way she had when the storm had at last brought rain to the dried-up garden but blown down the precious avocado tree.

Ti Jacques gave her the tourist money. The two boys gave Mama the pictures they had painted. She looked at them in surprise and shook her head. "Bon Dieu bon," she said. "God must know best."

Papa came out the door, his eyes fixed on the unsold sandals. The boys backed away. "One boy, trouble," he said angrily. "Two boys, double trouble."

"Tomorrow you can go yourself!" said Ti Jacques.

That was too much. "I'll teach you to talk that way to your father!" He had never beaten Ti Jacques before, but he was going to now.

From a safe distance, Ti Jacques hastened to explain. "I mean, tomorrow you can be a guide.

I have a real job for you, Papa!" The look in Gro Jacques' face changed slowly as he understood what Ti Jacques was saying.

"From now on I'll watch the ships, Papa. I'll watch the hotels for you. We will be partners!" added Ti Jacques.

"Never mind about the sandals then," said Papa. "I need a new pair myself, if I am to be in the city. The rest you can sell tomorrow, Ti Jacques, if you mind your business."

The next day before the sun was up, Gro Jacques and Ti Jacques, the new partners, set out for Port-au-Prince. Ti Jacques was carrying the rest of the sandals and a small basket of lettuce to sell for Mama. The city had never looked better to either of them. It was still so early that the shutters of the fancy wooden houses were still shut. Most of them had seen better days, but to Gro Jacques they were old friends.

At the hotel, people were beginning to stir. Through the window the two Jacques could see tables with white cloths being laid for breakfast. They waited in the lobby for the family Papa was

to guide. Ti Jacques was glad when they came, the children scrubbed and smiling. He was proud to introduce them to his papa.

Papa found a cab, and they all drove off, leaving Ti Jacques behind. He had two things in mind for the day: sell all the sandals and the lettuce, and then find more tourists. It was a lucky day for peddling, and by noon everything was sold. As he went toward the hotels, Ti Jacques noticed that the sky was getting dark. A strong wind began to blow. He ducked under an awning that was flapping wildly in the wind.

An old red and blue taxi-bus, called a camion, rattled to a stop close by. Amid claps of thunder, people climbed down from their perches on the roof of the camion to get inside it before the rain came. The driver was bringing out some cardboard boxes as big drops of rain began to fall.

A young man stood at the door of the taxi-bus, arguing with the driver. "You wouldn't put a newborn baby out in the rain, would you? Those are newborn babies in there!"

The driver said nothing. He stubbornly con-

tinued to bring out boxes and put them on the camion roof in the rain. The men and boys who had been sitting on the roof crowded inside. The young man looked very displeased. He took off his shirt and tucked it around the top box, but there was nothing more he could do.

Ti Jacques' curiosity got the better of him. Newborn babies on the top of a camion in the rain? He joined the crowd jamming into the camion. He would find out about that. He had his own money from the tire-changing in his pocket for fare, and he held the empty basket upside down over his head.

A large woman with a red scarf around her head held two squawking guinea hens above the crowd and shoved him onward from behind into a thin old man wearing a straw hat. Elbows jabbed him on either side.

"You are too nosy, Ti Jacques. . . . You are too nosy. . . . No good will come of it!" His mother's many warnings sounded as loud and clear in his mind as the sputtering motor of the camion sounded to his ears. But the warning was too late. The camion was on its way, and so was Ti Jacques.

32

Where? He did not know. But as the lightning flashed and the thunder roared, he worried more about the babies out there on the camion roof than about where he was.

The old camion clattered and swayed out of the city and into the hills. After a while the rain slowed down and stopped. The afternoon sun came out of the clouds. The camion jerked to a stop. Ti Jacques saw the young man pushing through the crowd, and he followed him out of the bus.

The young man lifted the wet boxes down from the roof with most gentle care. A weak peeping cry came from the round air holes in the boxes. When the last soggy box was lifted down, it fell apart. Out tumbled the babies—lots of them—tiny yellow and brown baby chicks! Some of them

33

stayed bedraggled where they fell. Some ran peeping into the long wet grass by the roadside.

Ti Jacques scrambled after them, careful where
he put down each foot. He combed through the
long grass with his hand to find the chicks. At last
all were huddled in his basket. The camion had
rattled on down the road, and only the young man
and Ti Jacques were left.

The young man shook Ti Jacques' hand. "Who
are you, and where did the wind blow you in
from?" he asked.

"I'm Ti Jacques. I was on the camion because
of the newborn babies."

"Well, would you believe it! I am George," said
the young man. "And these babies are one-day-old
chicks. Very special chicks. They came to Haiti
by airplane, and you helped save them."

Ti Jacques followed George with the basket of

peeping chicks on his head. Down a winding lane they went, through a banana grove and rows of tall corn. On either side of the lane were little bamboo huts on bamboo stilts, too small for people. Chickens were scratching in the doorways.

"What is this place?" asked Ti Jacques. He had never seen anything like it.

"We call this a cooperative," said George, "because we work together."

"Like we work together with our neighbors?" Ti Jacques looked around. He didn't hear any drums like when neighbors worked together on each other's fields at home.

"Where are the drums? Where is the feast?" he asked George.

"Chickens don't need drums," George told him. "We buy chickens together, and we sell them together."

"What happens to them in between?"

"Everybody takes some chickens home to raise."

That was something to tell Mama. She used to have chickens. Ti Jacques walked along the lane with his basket of chicks, George with the stack

of boxes. They entered a long, low building.

"Now I'll light this heater and dry the little guys off," George explained.

Soon the damp chicks were huddled under the big hood of the heater. Their peeping turned into contented chirps as they puffed out into brown and yellow balls of fluff.

"Now we'll go feed the chicks that came a week ago. They are about old enough to leave here." George let him help grind millet grain, corn, and papaya leaves into a mash for them.

"You sure did cooperate, Ti Jacques," George said, "so now you are in the cooperative." He picked out six of the fluffiest, liveliest week-old chicks and put them in Ti Jacques' lettuce basket.

"Take these chicks home. Build them a bamboo hut on stilts. In a couple of months they will lay eggs, bigger eggs than you ever saw." George gave Ti Jacques a small bag of mash. "Bring some of the grown chickens back here and exchange them for more little chicks."

It was late now, and Ti Jacques wasn't even sure where he was. Mama would be worried. Strange how days around the city were so much shorter than days at home. He was always getting fooled like this. But fortunately George was able to show him the shortest way over the mountain to his home village.

Ti Jacques was so happy he almost didn't notice how hungry he was. So friendly was the chirping overhead in the basket that he hardly gave Tonton Macoute a thought, even though it was almost night. "At last," he thought, "I have something for Mama. Vitale has his paints. Papa can be a

guide again. And now there is something good for Mama!" Ti Jacques would have jumped for joy had it not been for the chicks on his head.

When he finally arrived at home, it was late. Papa had come home long before. Mama was waiting for Ti Jacques. Her worries were over now that he had come, but she was not happy with him. Where had he been?

Ti Jacques gave her the sandal-and-lettuce money. He put the basket down beside the red coals left in the cooking fire. Papa, Mama, and Vitale looked into the basket at the chirping chicks and then at him, as if he were a magician. "They are for you, Mama." he said.

"Oh, Ti Jacques!" was all Mama could say. She put her hands into the basket, lifted out the chicks one by one and held them. They were the biggest and most beautiful baby chicks she had ever seen. When Ti Jacques had eaten the last of the beans and the big piece of pork fat Mama had kept warm for him, he told them his day's adventures.

Papa's day with the tourist family had been a good one. It was like old times to sit in the last

glow of the fire after a good supper and hear about his day in the city. "I guess I was too nosy again," said Ti Jacques. "I didn't find you a tourist for tomorrow."

His father laughed in the carefree way Ti Jacques remembered. "There is time for that," he said. "Tomorrow we must all build a bamboo hut for Mama's chicks."

40

Once in a while a quiet chirp came from the
basket, which Mama had already covered with a
woven mat and put inside the hut. The moon was
rising over the mountain, and it was bedtime for
all of them. As Ti Jacques lay almost asleep on his
banana-leaf mat with his sleeping family all around
him, he was content. In spite of himself, things had
turned out well.

41

ABOUT THE AUTHOR AND THE ILLUSTRATOR

Ruth and Allan Eitzen and their five school-age children recently took a lengthy summer vacation in Haiti. That provided the background for the story of Ti Jacques for Ruth Eitzen, and for the pictures of Allan Eitzen. Since then, Mr. Eitzen has returned to Haiti for further research.

After she graduated from college where she studied English, Ruth Eitzen worked four years in Europe with a church voluntary agency. Most of her writing has been for periodicals. She has also written and illustrated curriculum-related materials. Ti Jacques is Mrs. Eitzen's first children's book.

A native of Minnesota, Allan Eitzen attended college and art school in Minneapolis and Philadelphia. He left art school to obtain five years' "on-the-job" training with a religious publishing company. Mr. Eitzen subsequently finished his schooling and began a successful free-lance career. In his spare time he is remodeling the family's colonial farmhouse and taking part in historical drama.

Eitzen, Ruth   E
Ti Jacques, a story of Haiti

1974   4.12   3-5